BOOK OF MUCKROSS

Ooom Mucca Roose

Torc

John Allen

Palimpsest Annals not available in Trinity College Dublin

ISBN: 978-1-911345-12-1

Author: John ALLEN

Researchers: John Allen, David Allen, Sarah Allen

Editors: David Allen and Sarah Allen

Music: Sarah Allen

Printed and bound in Ireland by eprint limited

www.eprint.ie

To All The Original Words on

'The Isles'

That Were Never Listened

Gal Léó Gal Le Luí

Sarah Allen

Imram Chuairt a Mhéan Laethe
Síos Suas Trasna le Dteannta
Éan Amháin
Éin le Chéile
Sólas Ard is Ciunas

Translation:
Gal Boat Riding the Waves
The experience of a long journey at sea to our Dreams
Crossing the sea waves along the way
One bird joins with us
Then a flock of birds in chorus
The beauty of the sun shining and all
Around so quiet and peaceful
The nose of the boat rises on the waves
Then falls as the journey continues

'Mindsets'

Piis Ee-git	Piis Eegit	To Be
Ci feck	Feck	"To be,
deédeét feck	daye dayet feck	or not to be,
da fecker	da fecker	that is the question:"
Feck-di	Feck it	(blank)
(Homo sapiens the hunter)	(Kerryman)	(Shakespeare)
Up to 50,000 BC	21st Century	16/17th Century

History
Of
The Kingdom of Kerry

"Firdu gi ag riddi ooor

bayaal senos le gaal"

(Homo sapiens)

"Tá na fir ag rith go ooor

béal sionnan le gaal"

(Ancient Gaelic)

"The tribe are running fast

to the mouth of the Shannon for the gaal boat"

(English)

Prologue — Ooom Ooor

Since the limited publication of ten copies in velum hard back were released I have had time to reflect what I did. I believe I did what every former leaving certificate/A-level student of Gaelic/Irish always wanted (incl. Welsh, Scottish, Manx, Cornish) to decode namely 'what does this language really mean'? In this book I try to unearth a past that was a total unknown and into an unknown unknown, and I found it challenging and insightful and full of surprises that impacted to me the experience of a 'tomb raider'.

I imagined I brought my Irish/Gaelic dictionary into the science laboratory and during a demonstration of physics I brazenly casted it against electrons and what I saw were diffracting classical waves that looked so different from the original matter and yet the same. Connecting the dots with these thoughts of homo sapiens, our ancestors, and their words is extraordinary and insightful. This is what this compendium is about to rediscover my sovereign life and yours in Ireland and in the UK.

This experience even takes you to a word from a monkey learned by man and still found on 'the isles' making it the oldest known word in mankind. I had considered rebranding this commercial book and naming it 'Ooor' and incorporating the earlier edition 'Ooom Mucca Roose' and I believe that had this original language survived I would be referring to this piece I am writing as my 'ooom ooor' and not a 'prologue'.

Discovering these ancient words was an accident in the making after I undertook what I thought originally was a madness exercise to occupy myself in a Tea Room during the summer months of 2013 in Cashel, Co. Tipperary, under the shadow of the Rock of Cashel in Ireland next door to where my son was doing his university coop experience.

I would sit in a chair next to the entrance to the toilets with a large pot of tea and a warm gateau cake and cream on the table in front of me and beside them were dictionaries of the Wolof language from Senegal West Africa. I forensically examined each and every word slowly and attempted to relate it with Gaelic that I had learned at school. Some days I found none and other days found many.

Every word discovered felt like a gold leaf. It was tedious and slow and eventually it consumed me. I had no opinion before I commenced this arduous journey of enlightenment and the feeling was a journey to somewhere modern man had never gone before, a new perspective and a window of opportunity. It was a flight into the past through various galitical gravitational waves distorting time as we know it. Aptly the name of this traditional Tea Room shop was 'Spearman'.

It is difficult to know where I should start to share my afterthoughts so I have allowed the indulgence of my Starbucks coffee in the Citti of Lymericke to do that for me.

'SILE NA GIG' (P62)

This is the only spiritual practice I have discovered that homo sapiens and their primeval intentions have been continuously part of in this earlier fabric of suttee and cannibalism since their arrival from West Africa. A primal myth.

The islands of Inish Turk in the Atlantic Ocean off the west coast of Mayo, Ireland and in the centre of Lough Ree in the midlands are special places of mention that marked their sanctuary of spiritual adoration. Their animist worships eclipsed The Torah, The Bible and The Koran and only first encountered religion on the Isles of Britain and Ireland up to 50,000 years later when St Patrick (Celt) preached the gospels that subsequently subsumed their earlier beliefs to the control of Rome.

Today the Internet may have undone some of that success. To understand who was this figure (p46} of worship has remained a mystery until now. A copy of this solipsism resides in the local museum in Tralee, Co. Kerry masquerading as altruism in the past and a vernacular in the Kingdom

Nevertheless I am reminded of two myths. The first is – who is the real Satoshi Nakamoto – the founder of bitcoin, and why did Tom Hanks depict a sterile face only on a football in the film Caste Away.

Any enduring mystery made by man does drive up the values given to it by people whether it is a bitcoin or an icon. This human myth creates a scarcity that translates as a human need never to be replaced, especially when the supply is finite. This means a 'higher price' where greed eventually follows and high priests control the bounty. So far as we know homo sapiens left no written evidence and word of mouth was their only tradition that recorded their practices. Consequently organised religion conquered and replaced that tradition, and St Patrick (Celt) and his scribes with Rome reigned supreme, and this practiced written doctrine nowadays continues in organised religion today.

Similarly a disruptive force for incumbents to crypto-currencies has evolved into a greater enabler to the original bitcoins that initially suffered from government interventions because the original blockchain technology that it relied on was inferior. Subsequently new private blockchains – have been developed that has more control and arrests the lowering of the decline in profit banking ratio returns and might be sponsored by Goldman Sachs has created excitement about new prospects and become a new norm. A new Myth. Time will tell.

Sile na Gig is a succubus whose satrapy and followers decree it's mystery and purports to promote the practice of animalistic physical sexual intimacy and relationships as a spiritual expression to a higher self awareness of psychotic orgies and royal power. They recorded their practice in stone as a time capsule for future mankind. Homo sapiens brought the word 'sex' to the isles before white man arrived and its meaning has evolved since. Its original pronunciation may have been 'shex'.

Its derivative has continued today as a financial concubine preached by the high priests of banks and legislated by

dysfunctional regulations that can only deliver a lot of stark –
bollock naked Henrys and Paddies when the tide sweeps out
before the next tsunami hits and laughed at from every local
political pulpit. Corporate shareholders value being a
consequence of good business, not a prior objective, is the new
mantra while the interests of other stakeholders have little
traction. Ancient primal intimate gatherings can today perceived
be found in too many boardrooms and conspiring against the
public. Nothing has changed in the history humankind.

Does early man have a message, be it survival of the fittest or
otherwise and that lives forever and is durable and have other
new formal relationships now documented in deed in 'modern
times' have a longer term future. Will this ethical conundrum be
more suited to a financial advisor as a banker to an indebted
customer submerged in overvalued properties; or a priest in a
confessional box who pontificates behind a closeted partition the
virtues of hypocrisy? When will its secrecy be decoded in its own
Kerry Vatican ancient archives and by whom?

2. MINDSETS

Initially when you read the page 'mindsets' and prior to finishing the book, it feels dislodged with trepid imbecility. I should suggest that the reader should read Shakespeare's quotation first to be followed by Homo Sapiens <u>as if it was translated word for word linguistically in their ancient tongue</u>. Finally, read the quotation by the Kerryman 21st Century as being the translation of Homo Sapiens.

In that way you should record that similar animalistic mindsets between homo sapiens and the Kerryman have not changed since the dawn of mankind. Applying this forensic sequence is based on the order of things that the ancient words evolved in time and this is critical to understanding it's relevance today.

From this follows that the English words of Shakespeare which arrived from a source on the continent who's words were chiselled and honed with many other tongues over a very long time period that is almost incomprehensible in the timeframe approximate to modern man. The original words now used by Kerryman are untainted and unblemished and directly from the deep jungles in Africa. This makes this language unique on the isles of Britain and Ireland because it was once spoken throughout. This makes you feel like you are the richest sole broker operating inside the London Stock Exchange and be a 'cute hoor'.

History does not record the earliest demise of this Kerry Kingdom in the whole of 'the isles' or evidence of an interregnum in any period and we can only assume that a better armed force from the continent made that irrelevant to do then. It would be assumed that many assimilated and integrated into smaller distinctive cultural factions that were forced to form the nucleus to the various regions now still in existence i. e. Wales, Cornwall, Isle of Mann, Scotland etc.

The maxim 'If you do not know your history then you are doomed to repeat it', is relevant today in this modern world.

Currently UK and Ireland are members of the EU and this cohesive integration has strengthened in recent years. The story of the diverse scholarly mindsets in Ireland/UK, and the Charlemagne alliance (France & Germany) has never been addressed and yet is significant. The visibility presence within the high ranks of corporate, banking and political controls in the EU has declared very talented ex students from the Ecole Nationale Administratif and their alliances and are referred as the ENARCHY. Their mindsets are well placed to lead the future of Europe and the old schoolboy clubs of Oxford, Eaton and Trinity are destined to be eclipsed to a road of perdition. This shifting paradigm is a parallel to that ancient time period when the mindset of homo sapiens disappeared and replaced by Shakespeare.

Universities on the isles now need to address their philosophies to adapt or to become excluded from the new European club.

Empowered faceless unelected leadership from Europe, les immobilisme, induced powerless useless elected political leaders in Ireland and the UK, known as 'functionaires'. During the standoff in the banking crisis in Ireland in 2008-2010 their language was a humble Creole and their mindsets a potent mix of poisonous polonium. They won. The subsequent toothless Irish banking enquiry squirmed and the chorus 'that's all for now folks' resonated in the political corridors filling the pockets of their advisors for making smokeless Oireachtas/ parliamentary fuel.

The next show in town is the international corporate tax practiced in Ireland and being copied by the UK and promulgated as illusions by the Irish Government, the Irish tax professions and the qualified Irish accounting professions. Their might will be defeated by the proverbial wing of the small butterfly in the Amazon that has been marked 'enarchy' by the EU. International corporate investors need to decide which cover on the lid is real 'made in the EU' or 'made in The Isles'; before deciding a financial spoofed path into a vortex of Dante's inferno. The fate of their decision is final and that solution is not obvious and can never be re-drafted.

In decision theory and general systems theory, a mindset is a set of assumptions, methods, or notations held by one or more people or groups of people that is so established that it creates a powerful incentive within these people or groups to continue to adopt or accept prior behaviours, choices, or tools. This Kerry mindset is unique in that it remains the last and oldest embedded entrenched power group on The Isles and living in the south west corner of Ireland. This might explain why Daniel O'Connell, a barrister from south Kerry, delivered through his oratory skills the

Catholic Emancipation in Ireland that had endured 800 years of hardship and who was the precursor to the creation of The State (Republic of Ireland). What will define 'being Irish or British ' in the future order of things and will the primal Kerry mindset resurrect again and win.

Some questions we need answered include Do original ancient words found in Gaelic hold more creativity than subsequent benchmarked manmade fabricated bland versions as promulgated by The State (Republic) today? And does this Jungle fundamental animal mindset dominate our ways (the Irish) of thinking even if speaking English as a working language and having learned Gaelic at school? Does this mindset give us economic advantages in soft power that is mightier than *force majeure*? Do the Irish electorate vote for corrupt politicians more than any 1st world country and match the trends in African politics. Will this change and when? Do the Irish have more than 'luck' because their world can directly connect to ancient man being an animal and to be able to deliver that primal intuitive power lucidly? Is the current culture in Kerry 'a stain and/or a beauty' that cannot be removed from the fabric of the Isles of Britain and Ireland it once covered? Did the Stone of Scone originate in Kerry or Senegal and why does it hold regal magical powers used in Windsor? Perhaps it is now time that each kingdom exchange 'le seigneur des anneaux'.

3. Monkey business

The existential risk artificial intelligence poses to humanity today have seen soundings by those that create it – entrepreneurs; and is more fatal than nukes and may spell the end of the human race. The resurrection of algorithmic technology have enabled computers to engage in tasks only humans could do previously. This book shows a duality of how a significant word that imparted from a monkey to man was adopted into his language (Gaelic); and how man applied his reason in a science of logic that resulted in speed on water. It is a demonstration in essence and form of the close connection between logic and probability and indeed the dependence of the theory of probability on an underlying mathematical theory of logic. This is the earliest known proven mathematical doctrine of probabilities impacted by animal to man using a calculus of x, y and z where x = wing span of an eagle and y = boat and z the sound of the monkey. Its origins must have been between monkeys together when attempting to beating the odds to survive as species. Thus x+y+z = boat speed on water using a sail. Man used this law of composition to create his new technology and graduated this using multiplications to develop more and better. Thus x(yz) etc is more and better that leads to the best. Until then the axiom of mans' thoughts were idempotent and a contradiction in the same way Boolean theory was seen irrelevant when first written.

The monkey impacted nuanced differences in the laws of surviving in the jungle to man and their quality of pre-eminence was shown by their integrity in pursuit of the truth and stamped with a new primeval word of speech to feel that experience and how this created a new technology – speed that enabled homo sapiens to travel fast on water, the greatest marvel of its day.

Like speed artificial intelligence continues to outgrow itself using algorithms and soon an autonomous "superintelligence" programme will sneak up to humankind exponentially and pose a threat to humans. Perhaps a new defined cyborg humanoid will surpass humans, just as the homo sapiens did with the monkey, and forming new relationships of merging, mating and morphing with them. Either way the word 'ooor' has not disappeared from the evolution of manmade space technology and its Boolean like calculus was created and lives on in Gaelic.

4. DUBLIN BAY PROVENANCE

The mouth of the Liffey River needs more sticklers (innovative prudential tax policies) because nothing has changed since the arrival of homo sapiens to the shores of Dublin Bay. They adapt. What excitement they saw when they first set eyes on the breath of this fine bay upon arrival. To their primal eyes it was a bed of roses not needing any Viagra, fake boobs or Botox. It was their provenance. With their pure original homo sapien spirit of imagination and cognisance their myths held it all then and unblemished and untainted. Their new experience energised their innovative genius. They neologised the word Liffey to means 'a woman's vagina', Lambay Island to mean 'a bracelet ', perhaps to be attached and maybe it was at one time. The recent pharaonic global corporate mergers have re-invented this ancient innovative magic once more centralising tax provenance of world wide manufacturing operations and services and pleasures and never wanting ever to leave again. The sterling congo breath and hard breathing of homo sapiens will ensure a new inversion of product offspring like any carnivore to adapt and to populate once more a mighty sovereign on 'the isles'.

These mega events on world stage are now the hindsight of earlier primitive mans foresight with vision and their rhythm still holds and is not broken. Perhaps now it is a time of re-awakening from a long night before to find all the rewards arriving hatched from a dinosaurs egg. This ancient legacy continues and will grow and what arrives north of the Liffey will leave south of the Liffey, known musically in another time as Eblana Eblani (see

Ptolemy's Map) cycle of attractions, or in bland lay mans terms the business of importing and exporting.

The legacies from pure homo sapiens for Dublin Bay will continue, and to export their manhood and genius worldwide to the lesser morphed Neanderthal species elsewhere boxed in and capsuled and never to be forgotten.

The primitive lifestyle of homo sapiens shooting arrows to kill has now in their verb 'to stick' (see compendium) evolved to the present use of the word taxation, to be our sovereign throne; and modern mans hunting today in Dublin has revealed the new masters of the universe providing providence using an ancient primal art that the world needs, and that can be relied on in 'the isles'.

Today the capacity to gather information is increasing so is the likelihood of that information falling into the public domain as we have learned in recent times. Initially it begins as an encrypted code language that arrives to a respectable terminal and what follows is a need to publish to avoid it being scooped and what follows is a fall out from the revelation where 'the elite' are usually the victims in this process.

What may follow is a new myth from a global authority that will legislate 'to embalm' the evidence from future transparency to the public domain. Along the way the public suffer a cognitive limitation that will make it obtuse and obfuscated.

Homo sapiens in their time suffered raids on the spoils of their hunts and soon afterwards adapted to learn to protect their stock. The process of hunting and shooting arrows is the same as the process that tax is conceived and collected and that began on 'the isles' with their original words where their laws and infrastructures originated and today should remain to its tradition.

5. CLIMATE CHANGE

Were there Camels in Ireland? I don't know. However the current recorded ancient history of humankind shows no human recorded evidence of climate change in Ireland that is deemed significant to matter at all. In this book there is evidence that there was a recorded semi-desert by homo sapiens and is now covered with water and that this existed during human occupation because they recorded it. This place is Lough Neagh. Public records supports that Lord Shaftesbury extracts sand daily under licence to be used in the building industry, a current unregulated practice that would not be tolerated in UK. So what happened to cause this place to become flooded and why? Did primitive man live in this desert? Is the city of Atlantis buried underneath this sea of sand? Maybe not but why did water eventually cover the whole desert and is there a lost civilisation there, however small it may be. Should we know and will it teach us what we should know? This climatic event might have been known before but what was never known is that this happened after man arrived and was recorded then and makes possible to believe that more events like this will happen again and sooner than we think even now.

In Scotland Lough Ness derives its name from the presence of the 'flickering lights' of the aurora borealis. The contrasting names of the two close geographical lakes makes an interesting conversation and asks many comparative questions.

What comes next in a doomsday scenario on the isles? Unlike UK Ireland has no backbone central mountain range like the Pennine where all water gathered flows away from the centre to the seas laterally at various points. Instead the centre is flat and low lying and water gathers and remains there like a big wet sponge and the enormous excesses flows south known as the magnificent river Shannon making its waterway the largest and longest on the isles. Can this existing system continue to function today as we know it and will the people abandon it just like those who once lived in the desert under Lough Neagh.

Unlike the Netherlands the primary real threat of water is from within the lands and not from the ocean seas and is there such technology to protect the people and their businesses. Will we see a new 'delta economy' with canal boat transport returning once more and serving inland island communities under new national planning regulations. Perhaps all these questions are already answered in Europe and their bureaucratic operations will deem it fit that this chunk of the island of Ireland remains as a European national reserve only, to visit as a European Galapagos.

6. Bureaucratisation of Gaelic

(Tomas Mc Donagh Waldron — 'de Bhladraithe') & Germanic footprints Or Sterilising your Native Cognitive Skills

The 'mein kampt' of my early efforts to absorb Gaelic as a state school pupil was sterile and often frustrating and this subject never received the proper attention of my classmates either. Eventually, and that was only when I was about fourteen years old something changed. Puberty and good looking girls with intelligence made that possible. They were ambitious and I learned and we made good company together.

Speaking Gaelic in designated gatherings in the post Cromwell and Union Citti of Lymericke in the 60's was like experiencing another planet who's once ascendancy classes and Jews decided rightly to emigrate and left behind an empty famished void, of bronchitis damp sordid fouling derelict rumbling old tenement Georgian buildings filled with indentured desperate poor old pale skeletal ex bodacious maids and servants. After various solitary visits to the Aran Islands and living amongst the locals in their homes, on their boats, at their dances, sitting in their graveyards at night and visiting their pubs, collecting crabs, a normalcy happened. I connected to a new fabric in the ancient culture of Gaelic. I became free in their imaginary world floating in the Atlantic listening to the language of the boat people.

It is intended that this book be seen to embraces the interpretation of the 'original research papers and compendium' and that it can stimulate a spark of imagination for everyone who had to learn Gaelic or who's ancestors did and to contribute to the discussion of how we think on 'the isles'. This may determine should compulsory learning of Gaelic in school continue or allow the mindset of the people embrace the future or will the political fudging of academics/political self interests dictate the demise of this once ancient tongue to a vortex. The famous Swiss linguist Ferdinand de Saussure whose theory on the laws of sound is renowned for never wrote his book and it was the notes of his students that provided the basis of the research evidence that his theories represent. Trying to prove the correct meaning of a word by citing an earlier definition, or its Latin root, is spurious; language specialists call it the "etymological fallacy".

I have strived to see the surface and the underpinning complexity of form and medium the source of Gaelic presents by turning the downside up and in developing palimpsest-ing, laying layers upon layers, doing the archaeology of words in reverse bringing the bottom layer to the surface and in this way directly challenging and redeeming superficiality. This includes denouncing the existing anodyne tactic and challenging the stereotyping useless bauble of words borrowed by The State into Irish and to 'de – vladerise or de-waldronise ' part of that earlier myth and madness to make it pure. Challenging the false consensus effect promulgated by The State and political factions that consistently overrate the popularity of their cause is akin to recognising the truth that our brain is trained to ignore because their goal is to leave behind as many offspring as possible that will create a positive impression with their genes to future lost generations. In other words a future linguistic caliphate.

I had always believed that being human is that you're always in a constant transitional place. This free spirit I enjoyed came crashing down when I was writing this book when I realised that the recent direction of the evolution of the Gaelic language was removed from the west coast, where it had its spiritual home and was alive, and where many Gaelic poets found inspiration, and was now, in situ, in sterile government offices displaced from its origins and lost in a sea of jiu-jitsu linguistics in classroom politics that embraced the bureaucratic elite in the EU. It was now becoming a puppet language controlled by remote faceless third parties with strange names from foreign places and some only residing temporary in Ireland.

Nothing ever had prepared me for this collision and now I feel cheated after my sterling efforts in secondary school. My class mates in Ard Scoil Rís (1971) will feel the same too with a loud 'hurray' when they find out and so will many school pupils in the country. Perhaps the expression 'to Hell or to Connaught 'has a new meaning ' to listen to foreign faked words or the spirit of the real people from the West'

7. VISTAS

The Shannon river is the oldest surviving name given to any river in Europe and its earliest subsequent written record is shown on Ptolemy's map under the name 'senos'. This name is made up of two words from Wolof language meaning 'our water'. Its name derives from the Senegal River where both are magnificent vistas with an east-west direction flowing into the Atlantic Ocean and could be mistaken for each other on a sunny day and where the original homo sapiens departed from prior to arrival on 'the isles'. These people loved this estuary so much that they made it a family and a home calling various tributary rivers to be extended relatives and locations and safe havens to live, and the city rapids to be the experience of the excitement of their baby goats. They gave their first capital settlement on 'the isles' to the river island in the centre of the Citti of Lymericke to be 'the island for their boats'. From 'our gaal boat water (Senegal River) 'to 'our water' (Shannon Estuary) the two intercontinental rivers are entwined within the original mindsets of these people to be theirs on 'the isles' and the isles in the Citti of Lymerick. Subsequently to their arrivals they adapted their boats to the smaller rivers and shorter distances and for fishing, as explained in the compendium and all these boats remain part of the local tradition even today and celebrated in places like Newtown, Clarina, Co. Limerick.

FINALLY, allow me quote from my earlier book 'Da Wu Yu Code'

'The feeling of presence at the ring fort on the Aran Islands is one of before it was built; there was nothing. This period before man marked the earth was before time as we know it. Before time and throughout time, there has been a self existing being - eternal, infinite, complete, omnipresent. This being cannot be named or phrased, because human speech only applies to perceptible beings'.

In this book you will read has been found these perceptible beings and can name a man and woman Colin Buur Ruux and Ooor-la. He may have been a God of Abraham we never knew about and he may have sent his people into the desert from the Senegal river to travel by foot north into the Sahara. Maybe some did return and the others lost and maybe there are unknown unsung stories unwritten and unheard. Perhaps more Pharaohs have built more palaces and maybe somewhere under the wave of the desert sands lies a lost kingdom. We have not found his bible or commandments or golden calf but we do know how he and his tribe did think and how that has affected us today.

In conclusion, from the earliest times of arrival up to 50,000 years ago, and maybe more, nothing has changed since, and the mindsets of the people in Ireland today remain the same with those homo sapiens from Africa and are removed from those on the continent and the rest of the UK irrespective of what language is spoken together. History is repeating itself again. Migration continues to accelerate from the east and soon the sterile fabric remaining of the Celtic tradition will cease to be no more as we knew it but the mindset and vernacular will always reign supreme like a permanent unknown beauty and/or animal stain, from an unknown deep jungle; and living in a haven called Kerry.

READERS QUESTIONNAIRE FORUM

Q: Why did you write this book?

A: Until this information became available nobody else could have done this genre before.

Q: Is what you say relevant to today?

A: Our mindsets reflect the words we use and it is always important that we feel close to what those original words were intended for use. Language is a rhythm and that harmony must be maintained. It is not enough that we subscribe to myths and unproven scriptures. These new words speak in tongues.

Q: What do you mean by 'to conclude or be dammed '?

A: It is normal to be thinking and to be listened to. It is not normal to subscribe to the notion of being an 'agreeing machine' as opposed to a 'thinking machine'. I don't like to play the game of life of ' being stupid on purpose'.

Q: Is it not strange for a qualified accountant and taxation adviser to write this kind of book?

A: Technology allowed me the opportunity to turn an avocation into new ideas and print them.

Q: Do your findings show any relevance in current EU politics?

A: Yes.

Nothing has changed since after the arrival of homines sapientes to the isles of Britain and Ireland. They always learn 'to adapt'.

Subsequently to their arrival from west Africa was followed by early man from Europe up to 10,000 years BC, then the Romans, Battle of Hastings, Reformation, Napoleon, Hitler, and now the new integrated bureaucracy from the EU. These waves of attacks against the liberties professed on 'the isles' and the steadfastness of these islanders shows the alchemy of the unprecedented trust between man and man, islander and islander to remain unbroken and intact and to form part of the original mindset of homo sapiens and the Kingdom of Kerry that once ruled all the isles. Relationship with the EU is defined by continuity embodiment of a political conduct who's origins were first practiced on 'the isles' by homo sapiens from west Africa that evolved subsequently; moderation a self belief between islanders to survive as a unity with diversity; and separation original ancient social DNA is different on 'the isles' as explained in this book and makes the place unique.

The original social DNA of the Kingdom of Kerry and the House of Windsor have much more in common than we make it out to be. It is now time to write it down and live by it.

Q: Is there an Identity Crisis on 'The Isles'?

A: Yes

Where/When was the first Kingdom of The Isles... I don't think anyone knows and official history does not record it and why? Unofficial history in this book does and that is why it is unofficial but you don't know that because academic Ireland, the perceived surrogate, will not allow their ignorance be seen and to share pro-actively with academia elsewhere on 'the isles'. We see Windsor as the rightful seat of unity and I do not dispute but who were their original precursors? This missing key tout court will dictate what lies ahead and not the scattered chieftains of the workplaces. The language may be engaging and changing within a debate but the mindsets never change and remains durable and always prevails.

Tribal responses within 'the isles' to articles and debates are divisive and allow hostility to flourish bankrolled by various foreign vested interest that do not subscribe to free speech or liberal opinions.

So why is crisis of identity on the isles in real danger because we made it happen and voters will go to the booths armed with their prejudices, presumptions and their fear of the future.

Q: If the inverse occurred and homo sapiens were found alive somewhere on the isles, are there any words in your compendium that they might find confusing or how would they feel in today's world?

A: They would think that the name Ryanair to mean 'laughing gas'.

They would wonder why many words currently used by modern man on the isles have no known natural origins in their meanings both in Gaelic and Hiberno Irish and are just invented myths without a proper constructive thought process. They would perceive this as a suppression in social engagements for the ordinary people by the elite.

They would be glad to see that their own original technology in their alcohol cum derivatives e. g. 'whiskey', and many of their own 'boats' are still flourishing and that the 'Poc Fair'in Killorglin, Kerry continues in their memory and that they can view 'Síle na Gig' in the museum in Tralee.

They would wonder why so few people have pursed lips and how they cannot properly pronounce the words Ooom, Ooor, Buur and Ruux.

Body smells from modern mans daily flatulence would be so different to theirs so foods would be a suspect.

Q: Can you perceive the perceptible beings these Ancient homo sapiens were in our human history?

A: Yes.

Every effort has been made to make it possible for the reader to comprehend and to demonstrate how much in common modern man today shares with them. It is reasonable to assume the earliest names used by homo sapiens on 'the isles' Colin Buur Ruux for a man, and Ooor La for a woman.

Q: Do we now understand more about the physical landscape in Ireland?

A: Yes.

Water is eternal and government policies are not. The research includes the revelation during a time when homo sapiens occupied the island of Ireland that there was a semi desert in a place that is now a lake known as Lough Neagh (see compendium). This information indicates trends that there will be more water from within the country as well as around the island and their levels will rise and create a labyrinth of deltas and new boating communities. Selected cities and towns will have to be reinforced and others abandoned. Our bogs are more recent than originally thought. Also there is more gold and precious metals to be found on many of our rivers and there may be a lost civilisation underneath Lough Neagh.

Q: Is there anything else you might like to say?

A: Yes.

Man originally conceived the Internet from a word imparted from the monkey to mean speed and this word was 'Ooor'.

Human beings weren't built for progress – maybe a bit of change here and there, a bit of adaptability but not for what we are now collectively enduring; a non-stop trapped – inside – the –future nagging buzz we all share in the 21st century where uploading and downloading is a norm. No animal is built that way. The longing for a pre-internet brain will endure and only to be found by reading a book or living in the wilds. Today there is an inflection point where the propensity of robot inference in our lives will expand exponentially beyond our comprehension in the immediate years. There was also an inflection point when homo sapiens parted from the monkey and evolved and soon the dexterous robot will take our place and man will remain just man either free or indentured.

Q: You have shown examples of words used in Hiberno English to originate from homo sapiens in West Africa do you have any more?

A: Yes.

1   Bejaysus This means - (Wolof) 'The sudden appearance of a goat '.

'béy' (Wolof) = goat

'jaas' (Wolof) = sudden.

Today meaning the sudden surprise of meeting someone you might know.

2. Begorrah This means – (Wolof) 'You are noble'.

'be' (Wolof) = to is, are

'gor' (Wolof) = noble.

Today meaning to refer to someone that is looking great.

3 Effen This means -(Wolof)'to call someone usually a man's attention and within a tribe to load something on the head of someone'. This was and still is a normal way to carry things in Senegal especially by women.

'Ee' = to call someone (Strong vowel)

'en' = to load on head

'f' =(silent) tribe member as in 'fir' see compendium.

'They couldn't get it into their head'. Today it is still commonly used and now can mean trying to understand someone who may have made a simple mistake.

Q: Is there anything else?

A: Recently I met a lady in Starbucks at Limerick Railway Station who holds a PhD in the sciences of fungi. She was on her way to a conference in Dublin to make a presentation. She told me that modern man in the western world have less fungi in their bodies than they did in the past and are now more vulnerable to disease than before. I thought this was interesting. It makes sense that if we have more fungus we are more able bodied.

If we try to imagine that the original words in the compendium had more fungus than the bland bureaucratic verbatim proclaimed by The State maybe there would be more life in the language we are trying to fake. A phial of pure carbon will make you a sparkling diamond but don't try anything else. To quote 'the selfish gene theory is clear that a species could not care less if its survival techniques are useful or a detriment to others, provided that any benefit or injury bestowed does not prove a handicap to its own survival'.

Q: Anymore?

A: The real problem today on 'the isles' is that nobody can define the word 'tax'. Everyone think 'they know' and what they say limits the opportunity to make it work on the international markets. Their response is to an 'operative process'. Pragmatism is not the answer on its own. Something more accountable and transparent shows the light. This compendium is the beginning of that experience.

Fundamentally the absolute need to survive to hunt must be the cornerstone to be re-claimed and done 'in deed'. Losing the willpower to do this noble act will deny the place, the product and the hunter… and that translates to mean 'society' as we know it. This rhythm of evolution must not be broken.

Tax is a provocative word by design and purpose and is not a myth. It needs 'an urge' to enable to be enabled to fuel the challenge to be successful. Finding an ambergris would be a good start. This experience should embrace an unpropitious air of attraction that when inhaled the experience is never forgotten. Even though its ingredients may be seen to be vomitus and faecal its alchemy transfers into a rich perfume that attracts a high market value in society for the exchequer and fills a royal chrism that is good enough for a coronation.

In the absence of 'an urge' there becomes a void to be filled by a nearby tribe and the resulting societal edifice collapses to subsume to a new authority. To fuel the challenge to the deed, 'the urge' maintains the status quo and Dublin is the place.

Q: Posthumous Brexit?

A: Read more.

Table of Contents

Prologue – Ooom Ooor.. i

Readers Questionnaire Forum... xxiii

Preface.. 1

Introduction.. 2

To Conclude or Be Dammed 5
   Lexicon of Royle Couched Words... 7
   Who Made The World?.. 9
   Words of Feathers 18
   Faustian Pact 27
   Tinnitus in Words.. 31
   Conspectus 35

Language is a Currency 37

Compendium of the Oldest Words on the Isles of Britain &
Ireland 39

Ptolemy's Map of Ireland 40

Trends 76

Deciphering the Speed Graph 83

Historical Background 91

'The Isles' - Ireland & Britain 95

Ptolmey's Maps 99

Senegal & Gambia 101

The Human Journey 105

Hunters Law of Nature.. 107

Black America 111

Taxation – Brief 1 & 2.. 115
   Taxation Brief 1 115
   Taxation Brief 2 116

Back to the Beginning... 119

Glossary 123

Addendum.. 125
   Da Wu Yu Code (extract from the book)............................ 125

References.. 130

Preface

Walking the long beaches in Senegal and Gambia and listening to the ebb and flow of the waves of the Atlantic Ocean, there is an ever presence of something familiar. Looking into the vast ocean something resonates within.

I have walked many times the long sandy beaches of Ballybunnion, Co. Kerry, when the tide was out and the music played by the tides was the same tune and rhythm and with possibly the same baton.

There is an eerie sense of presence in both places that is recognisable to be the same and the chorus played holds in harmony the full stretch between the two continents.

Somewhat further out the colourful Puffin bird passes by making its own sound that makes this ocean unique.

INTRODUCTION

Language today is in a constant state of flux and the same words can often have different meanings depending on when they were used in history. Recently some words have changed their meanings unrecognisably and would have different meanings today depending on the age group and the person expressing them.

I have discovered a substrate language to old Irish (Gaelic) where some of the words are still used today. These words predate the arrival of the Celts into Ireland and Great Britain and arrived directly from Africa, thus untainted and unblemished and without discourse to other cultures. These are among 'the originals' in ancient mans mindset and no other major European language includes them in the same way.

As a result it is possible to identify the original intentions of ancient man when first the words were coined or 'clicked' in some cases. This is a eureka moment hatched from a dinosaur's egg and could be delivered into the courts chambers to be dissected on the floor.

In this book the words could be older than 50,000 years and unchanged and from when man was primitive and when survival of the fittest only continued their destiny. Maybe some of those in Ireland are part of them. Maybe more of them in America both Black and White. Maybe these words offer us hope.

It is intended that this evaluation should initiate further study and that what does flow may mankind reap it in abundance.

To Conclude or Be Dammed

The Jury in any court of law represent the law of the land and it is their decision that must be listened to and accepted. Likewise the electorate decides who represent the nation's politics.

To conclude requires a process of listening and assessment, both together. Otherwise there would be a societal weakness whose ballast would cause to topple at some point.

Many decisions are based on beliefs concerning the likelihood of uncertain events in life that either have or may have happened or might happen in the future. Occasionally, beliefs concerning uncertain events are expressed in numerical form as odds or subjective probabilities… such as betting and going to the races.

This short simple book attempts to define these convictions and in doing so refutes the heuristic principles (rule of thumb) adopted by the elite in universities when examining this presentation and evidence and when theirs only leads to severe and systematic errors. They are making judgements, in this context, on their data of limited validity processed according to irrelevant heuristic rules. The evidence in this presentation has never been revealed before yet alone discussed.

This judgement to conclude tries to simply rationalise these decisions and to embrace the people's belief what they believe they feel and who live in the real world.

This conclusion is an affront to the conventional wisdom of the entrenched hypothesis on the linguistics and laws of sound insofar as they infringe on these findings.

The goal of what you are reading is to demonstrate that the tenets are true and that any reading of the texts in this compendium would be 'valid', since any reading would correspond to what the text 'says'.

"A word sequence means nothing in particular until somebody either means something by it or understands something from it. There is no magic land of meaning outside of human consciousness. Whenever meaning is connected to words, a person is making the connection, and the particular meanings he leads to them are never the only legitimate ones under the norms and conventions of his language. "

By: E. D Hirsch Jr.

LEXICON OF ROYLE COUCHED WORDS

Can we be too secure to ask where did our ideas and how we think came from and what words are relevant and why? Complacency and even indolence induces a false security in oneself. Do we believe that by searching for new meanings to 'an established word set' may give rise to a feeling of insecurity and a judgement that someone else might make?

Feeling secure in oneself is a rich experience and encourages self-reliance by believing in our ability to cope and not restrained by anxiety or lack of ability. We must not ignore our fundamental vulnerabilities and the dangers associated with feeling excessive security and relying on 'others powers and strength'. Questioning the infallibility of others must be a cornerstone to our cultural longevity that can only eventually enrich us as a nation and embrace healthy economics. Failure to do that numbs joy, happiness, and gratitude.

Believing that the revelations in these new words and their original meanings in this compendium will contribute to the foundations on which we build our lives and will encourage us to makes this in rock and not on sand.

This can be seen as a new philosophical stone to build on and offers more resources and opportunities for others to research and discover and make the Isles of Britain and Ireland a more interesting place than what we already know.

Our ideas of truth and knowledge learned from this compendium will match the insecurity of truth and falsity and right or wrong and remove all the numbness we have had to date.

We have to accept that what we believe might be false, what we do in good faith might be wrong, what we make most real might be an illusion. At the same time, we must do our best to get as close to the truth and good and the real as we can. Philosophically, we are walking a tightrope, thinking without a safety net.

WHO MADE THE WORLD?

I hope God did.

Where is God? That's a good question.

I know when my son was a young boy we used to look for Wally, a comic character. He was on every page but we still had to find him, and we did. Finding Wally was a game. So, 'Wally is on every page'.

When I was young Denis the Menace was the person at large then. He had cousins and friends such as Desperate Dan and Beryl The Peril. They absorbed my energy in my youth and gave me lots of ideas. When my son has his own children who will Wally's next of kin be and where? My guess is he will be in the clouds and not on the pages. So complicated everything becomes. Soon Wally's son will only be in the clouds and not on the pages. Oh technology changes everything. So does language.

Wally was English. I have never known an Irish Wally. As usual everything I am informed about arrives from the east coast through media. That includes Dublin, London and the EU. This forms all the channels of our bureaucracy as we know it today in Ireland. Why not from the west coast of Ireland?

As a result of bureaucratisation in our daily lives nobody has the time to think what is good for themselves and as a result life passes and time changes. The Irish language under the stewardship of The State changes too because that is what languages do. Unknown to most of us the control of its true original origins in Ireland lies with people that have lived elsewhere other than Ireland and never with a native west of Ireland qualified Professor of Ancient Irish. Why are they not holding this esteemed office where it really matters? Are they the victims of 'total bureaucratisation' and stunted to behave as the 'perfect student' for an entire lifetime? Does the experience of operating within a system of formalised rules and regulations, under hierarchies of impersonal officials, hold a kind of covert appeal?

There is a school of thought that holds that bureaucracy tends to expand according to a kind of perverse but inescapable inner logic. The argument runs as follows: if you create a bureaucratic structure to deal with a problem, that structure will invariable end up creating other problems that seem as if they, too, can only be solved by bureaucratic means. In universities, this is sometimes informally referred to as the "creating committees to deal with the problem of too many committees" problem.

A slightly different version of the argument is that once bureaucracy has been created, it will immediately move to make itself indispensable to anyone trying to wield power, no matter what they wish to do with it. The chief way to do this is always by attempting to monopolise access to the certain key types of information. As Max Weber, one of the greatest German scholars of the later 19th and early 20th centuries, writes: 'Every bureaucracy seeks to increase the superiority of the professionally informed by keeping their knowledge and intentions secret... in so far as it can, it hides its knowledge and actions from criticism. Once created it is hard to get rid of it. The only real way to rid oneself of an established bureaucracy according to Weber, is to simply kill them all, as Alaric the Goth did in Imperial Rome, or Genghis Khan in certain parts of the middle east. Leaving any significant numbers of functionaries alive and, within a few years they will inevitable end up managing ones kingdom.

In the upper echelons of the Irish public sector and most 'respectable people', believe that unless any language found to originate from the west coast including Kerry needs to have a correlation with Indo European languages first and always first with no exceptions and this is their conventional wisdom. Even if the discovery originated to belong to a much earlier period predating the Indo European family of languages. This does not make sensible logic. This is like comparing chalk and cheese and expect them both on the menu.

When bureaucracy ideas becomes a conventional wisdom, it is extremely difficult to change it, because many so-called 'serious people' have lined up behind it.

As the wonderful economist JK Galbraith noted, when "serious people" are faced with the choice between changing their minds and finding the proof that there is no need to do so, they invariably get busy looking for the proof'.

As a result there is no debate, and those who suggest that the emperor has no clothes are dismissed as mavericks or cranks – or, worse still, they are accused, in the ultimate putdown deployed by serious people, of guess what? Not being serious.

But this is deadly serious. Because there is no way we can foster our real language and real culture where it truly matters and claim it to be ours. Or better still to make it ours.

So who benefits? Clearly those people who are well paid in very senior civil servant positions entrenched in secured gold minted positions and they do not want their conventional wisdom to change even when it should.

The Rising of 1916 is a celebration of freedom in Ireland and the General Post Office in Dublin was the centre of this location and also the centre of gravity where all national bureaucracy is networked from what was originally modelled from Germany and its Deutsch Post system. It could be argued that the insurrection might have been an attack on bureaucracy that had its origins in Germany under a peaceful social order. Partition resulted and the dissidents known as republicans became divided and all in the name of bureaucracy and how it should be run.

There was a time in the middle ages when Kerry became divided too between north and south and the dividing line was the river Maine in the centre of the county. Even religion was not part of the reason because this was during a period before the reign of Henry VIII.

It had its origins in the House of Plantagenet in the north of England and under the local tutelage of King John in Lymericke Citi. Families such as the Fitzgerald's, Mc Elligott's, Blenerhassets, Enrights, Hayes, Buckleys, Harmon, Daly etc were part of those settlers and they remain there today. Maybe religious bureaucracy and feudalism was... all in the name of bureaucracy of course. Bureaucracy brings its own language. This Kerry Schism is still in the memories of the natives old enough to remember. This can still be observed during weekly local Gaelic matches between opposing regions of this river and they ensure the referee is not from Kerry. Marriages inter-regions and 'the talk' have been stories for many years and their gossips still flourish. Rebels in the south always mark their presence by maintaining control of their own independent international banking activities within their corporate fiefdom. Soon, if not already, they will be mining the abundance of gold and precious metals in the Beara Peninsula. Why has The State not done this before when ancient primitive man did?

Up the Rebels is a South Kerry chorus. Where did the liberator Daniel O'Connell come from? It is ironic that the GPO was situated before the insurrection in Sackville Street in front of Lord Nelson monument and now renamed O'Connell Street. How many times have Kerry locals living in Dublin returning home by car have to stop once they cross the regional imaginary border and into the town of Castlemaine for a pint knowing then only they were now finally at home before they can continue onwards to where they once lived. It is still written in their psych. Funeral hearses do the same as if they reached the gates of heaven before burial. There were rebels in North Kerry too but they had to quickly skirmish across the Estuary to Clare and remain there. Why is the surname 'Tubridy' from Kilrush, Co. Clare when that name had its origins in a village in North Kerry aptly named Tubridy? And there are others. It would be interesting to see the

13

notes of the local functionaries 'The Barney Cops 'who imposed the new bureaucracy in the name of feudalism and religious Norman bureaucracy and those names they held. These bureaucrats were known as Normans who mainly hailed from below the Hadrian Wall in north of England and who carried the loyalty of their own fiefdom to North Kerry.

The said evidence of the substrate Gaelic language came from the west and this forms the origins of what made Kerry in the first place and where it goes from here on after. Bureaucracy must not be allowed to stunt a regional opportunity for the people that now live there.

Bureaucracy mirrors the same banking system failure that was allowed to happen in Ireland in recent times and will this bring another insurrection or rising on the island or will it be war decided by others? Revelations in the Irish banking system have now been proven to have been corrupt. This makes the rest of our national bureaucracy a suspect too.

What language does the Minister for Finance speak when he promotes the sale of all unpaid household mortgages to unregulated foreign controlled vulture funds, without recourse to being allowed to appoint their own appeal commissioner, and not a nominated Minister clad one. The new revelations in these words of primitive man shows that there is indeed a difference in meaning of the two separate words 'Tax' and 'Cáin' in the Finance Acts and on a broader level the actions of the Minister are in breach of his fiduciary duties in public office.

Today the Internet with e-mail and national post code is a giant super-efficient post office. Has it not, too, created a sense of a new remarkable effective form of cooperative economy emerging from within the shell of capitalism itself, even as it has deluged us with scams, spam and commercial offers and enable the government to spy on us in new and creative ways? Military tactics used in peaceful times!

Since the creation of the new Irish Taxi Regulatory Authority it has been noticed that Irish taxis must show a designated emblem properly inserted by authorised personnel on the vehicle and that the words shown to be either 'Taxi' or 'Tacsaí'. So for the first time there are two separate words for taxi as we once knew it. An e-mail to An Forus Gaeilge to request the meaning of this word 'Tacsaí' was sent and this was their written response:

"The word tacsaí has been used in Irish since at least 1959, when it was included in De Bhaldraithe's English Irish dictionary. It was likely a direct translation of the English word, which it seems was based on the Latin taxare' 'to levy a fee'. The word would not be used in Irish as it is an English word and there is no reason to use an English word when speaking or writing in Irish unless it is trademarked and cannot be translated".

Their logic is confusing. Especially when they imply that they have never known a previous Irish word for taxi and just because they claim it is an English word then the word is wrong to use. Maybe this has something to do with the 1916 GPO proclamation. A Latin word, so they say, seems an 'ok' acceptable fashion to adopt. It still makes nonsense. Just imagine foreigners never before in Ireland sees a sea of 'tacsaí' and taxis, they cannot be blamed for thinking that they might be in Rome making a choice that is challenging the black economy and Irish credibility factor.

So is the word Taxi an English word? The evidence presented in this compendium shows that the word Tax and Cáin are both Wolof and from Africa? Why is The State calling bluff? Taxi is a Gaelic word and more importantly a Kerry word. The world should know that. So is Irish dancing originally part of Kerry culture before anywhere else on the island of Ireland or Britain. We need a crier to tell those who substrate us and to listen to what we have to say.

Also in Germany, one could make the argument that the nation was created more than anything else, by the Deutsch Post. Under the Holy Roman Empire the right to run a postal courier system within imperial territories had been granted in good feudal fashion, to a noble family originally from Milan, later to be known as the Barons Von Thurn and Taxis. One later scion of this family was the inventor of the taximeter, which is why taxi cabs ultimately came to bear his name.

So who do we now believe? Is Foras na Gaeilge an organ of the EU or a voice of the people from the West Coast of Ireland? Is 'Irish' now a partitioned language claimed only by bureaucrats and the EU to be eventually disposed to the ether, a nothing. Are we crumbling in the face of bureaucratic grumbling?

Unless those that hold Gaelic to be a part of their conviction think clearly and make The State accountable for the true origins of their language that is seen to work then their fate as a people is no more and the Deutsch Post System masquerading as the GPO will substitute theirs for ours thus all we once had becomes a substrate into a new order of words in the future. We will become a foreigner in our own lands like the original Black man did when he encountered White man after many earlier years of settlement. History will have repeated itself once more.

Then .... who made the World?

A Black Kerry Man.

Where is 'he'?

GONE........... but he might come back as a President ...of a country or a hedge fund system or .... singer ...dancer ...does it matter?

Now .... who made the World?

A Very Senior Civil Servant.

Where is 'he'?

Dublin/London/EU .... a Trilogy ...funded with buckets of tax free expenses and living a high life in leafy Dublin ......soon to be pensioned off and replaced all over again.

Words of Feathers

I am neither a writer nor an academic nor am I fluent in the Irish Language or Wolof. I can listen but I find it difficult to hear. I want to provoke you to think your words through.

Before you continue to read further there are obstacles you must encounter. These include credibility, proof of what I write and being realistic how the words I show you began with man. Particularly since the first man on 'The Isles of Britain and Ireland 'was BLACK.

After completion of my earlier draft I wanted to meet with those in authority in Ireland, who are paid very high salaries in many Irish Language Government Bodies, to explain my findings. My experiences were profound. None would accept that they held the remit to discuss the matter and that included the Department of the Irish Prime Minister and the Irish Language Commission. The Department of Education proposed various Irish Universities to contact.

I did, and Trinity College Dublin refused to meet me and after I persisting and sending them a script of words the administrator only responded by e-mail informing me of the following: 'Sorry for the delay. He has indeed come back to me and I'm afraid that he was very negative about the submission. He said that the rigour of comparative linguistics had not been applied and the emphasis was on superficial similarities between words rather than clear linguistic correspondences amenable to explanation by sound-law theory. He pointed too to a number of errors in the interpretation of Irish words. No attempt was made, he pointed out, to look at early forms of Irish to establish the shape of words at the most relevant time, particularly in the interpretation of surnames but not only there. '

I persisted in wanting to meet TCD only to be told in writing to go to a Catholic University. I did and was told the same. Suffice to say that they agreed that my findings could be true and it was possible and the words did show resonance in the Irish Language and they wanted proof using their academic unproven man made hypothesis as a tool to prove my claim. Their accusation to me is that I concluded without using their hypothesis. If you search the Internet there are many qualified academic objectors that denounce their imposed obscure techniques. My findings would have the support of Ferdinand Saussure, the father of linguistics, because his theories are based on the premise that a language is based on a 'collective product of social interaction' and the words used in this compendium never had this discourse therefore his science is not relevant to these peripheral findings shown in this book. What I did find very interesting is that very many of the nominated relevant persons on authority on ancient Irish had strange and eastern European sounding names and were impossible to make contact with. Many with Irish sounded names evaded my approaches. It may be now appropriate to quote Edward Lorenz:

Chaos
When the present determines the future,
But the approximate presence does not
Appropriately determine the future.

Our languages followed humans in a natural way. The sensitivities of predictions made by academics to uncertainties of the current knowledge of human behaviour over a large timescale are a fundamental point and are unstable. The uncertainty is down to the extreme sensitivity of the predictions that is called the initial condition. Academics have made fundamental errors by assuming that it was not possible for early humankind to leave Africa along the West Coast. They have failed to find evidence and their existing records do not hold the findings as in this compendium. Perhaps their reason was that there was no river in a north south direction that would take man through the Sahara Desert as the Nile did on the East Coast. Maybe they could not find fossils to support evidence and how could they when primitive man went by boat and fossils might have gone overboard. In any event the earliest technology was wood only that is not durable to last long. The findings in this compendium do create a human axiom that cannot be contradicted. There is simply no other rational choice than to act according to the best available science, imperfect though, by necessity, its predictions will always be.

I did receive a letter from The Queen of England and The President of Ireland confirming they had received my compendium on the First Words Spoken on the Isles of Britain and Ireland.

One day I met a legal academic in a beautiful coffee shop zest beside the park in Limerick and we held a discussion. I explained to him what my findings were based on. I related to him the following:

'There are very well known web sites that confirm to show how man migrated in a journey from South Central Africa 160,000 years ago and how man travelled along the Nile river through the Sahara Desert and onwards and inhabited the world and that this migration forms the bases on which the current body of knowledge on languages as we know them have been taught and understood. http://www.bradshawfoundation.com/journey/ I confirmed that I agree with this and do not want to change these facts. This source also states that white man arrived on the Isles of Britain and Ireland from Continental Europe around 8,000 years BC. I do not dispute this either.

He intervened with a sense of disapproval to say: 'What are you trying to say then, John?

My body language and my efforts reasserted themselves to locate a podium at the table and respond. This is what I had to say:

'If you look at the initial movement from this Original Garden in Africa people left to travel in three directions. There were those who travelled along the Nile River, those to the West and those to the South. My story to you is about those who travelled towards Senegal along the Atlantic Coast. The current official records show they stopped there and remained. They could not travel any further north because there was no river flowing in the north direction as did the Nile. The desert was too hot, too big and too dangerous. I believe subsequently they travelled by boat to the Isles of Britain and Ireland many many thousands of years earlier than White man.

He responded: 'How can you prove that'?

I replied: 'I know all their boats that either reached and or they developed in Ireland because they all have African words and form part of Gaelic today '. There are at least six. These include a trend of words. They also brought Irish Dancing, The Irish Goat Fair in Kerry, Ogham Stones, names on Ptolemy's Map, Place Names, names in politics and the surname of Brian BORÚ'.

His face grimaced and felt a sense of discomfort and surprise and said: Look........ . em...John. 'Listen' ...'John'. This is how I see it. Try to imagine that you are in court and you are claiming that 'Jack' owes you €200,000.

I intervened. 'That might only be €200 or at most €2,000. €200,000 is too much'.

Listen John he says: 'Its €200,000. OK?

'Ok'.

'Now you say to the Judge that you did the work and Jack says you did not and it is your word against his. The Judge is likely to agree with Jack and you lose.

I said: 'I agree'. 'But'.

'But what?' 'Now listen, John. You have no answer for this. I mean it so stop '.

'I am serious', I retorted. 'I do have an answer to your query'. 'You see in my case, Jack never appeared in court to hear my claim and even though subsequent attempts were made by order of the Judge to demand his attendance Jack failed to turn up. The Judge in this case subsequently gave an order that my claim is valid. So I won. As I said before nobody has attempted to study and research the journey from West Africa to Ireland. My conclusions are real for now because there is no reasonable alternative on record. All that is offered are qualified assumptions and possibilities without relevant material. Mine is different because mine have relative facts that are significant and there is no alternative contest to these 'now'.

'Ok', he says, 'you have proven it in the example I have demonstrated. But how does your claim in the language findings of yours fit into the idea that Jack did not turn up in court?

'It's simple. In the realm of the best knowledge available to date by all academics it is accepted that there is no evidence available to show on the Isles of Britain and Ireland where the earliest man came from prior to the years 8,000 years BC and the most they can say is to speculate and assume. But clearly they have admitted they have nothing to support and even their assumptions which are only speculation'.

'So you assume they all came by boat from Senegal to Ireland and that is your claim'?

I know they claim by boat it is my instinct that tells me. 'YES'.

'Why did these Idiots in the Departments in Government not study this before? Don't answer, they were too well paid to move their ARSE. They Don't Want To Listen '?

'Exactly'.

'They are like the bankers. Bloody Buggers'.

'Yes, I agree and they are choking the potential of the language to be absorbed voluntarily by the people by restraining and constricting it to lots of useless unproven hypotheses.

'Explain'?

'Ok. What I am claiming is that this original language arrived in Ireland directly many many thousands of years earlier perhaps at least 25,000 years and more and without discourse with other languages because this language held its African originality in its purity as they travelled along the Atlantic. This forms the words I have found. My assertion is that the hypothesis used by the academics to insist that the original African words I have found to have been linked with the Indo European Family is groundless. In addition their insistence of my comparison meanings with existing Irish words are also groundless because this 'Irish' is Celtic/Indo European and my words that I call Gaelic have separately their own original African roots.

'Do we speak them today'?

'These words form the substrate language prior to the arrival of The Celts and have been absorbed into the Irish language we use today'.

'Amazing'. 'I cannot believe it'. 'Will you have another Flat White Coffee'?

'If you pay for it'.

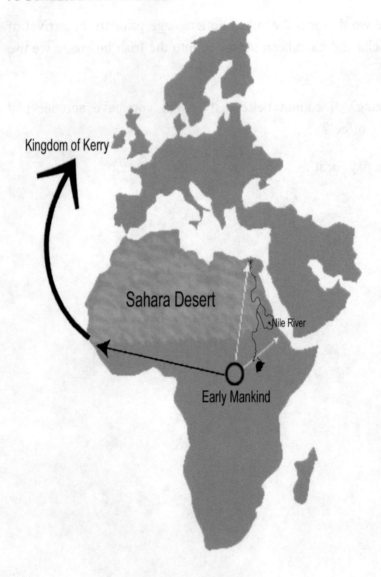

The Untold Human Migration

FAUSTIAN PACT

The Islands of Ireland and Britain are completely surrounded by seas. Separately and together the seas and oceans wrap them into a slumber of betrothal and their periphery islands dangle like decorations or orbitals depending how politics flows and their economic consequences. A faraway island can be nearer to Westminster Parliament than London Bridge if a sheep farmer on Orkney Island wants to change its flag. The oceans are perceived as out of this world due to their sizes and depth and the consequential dangers associated with it. Yes, fear does create its own borders too and that fine line between the physical and imaginary can be fraught with difficulty. Continental Europe is simply land to go to should the islands begin to sink or float away or to evade the law. We imagine that people travel to and from the continent over the seas only and that is what history has recorded. Oceans are not for the fainthearted and early history does not mention it. However monks have been known as early navigators and may have landed in the Americas. Before that time there is nothing absolutely nothing we know.

We need to understand that the Atlantic Ocean is big. I mean big as in 'mighty big' and almost surrounds the island of Britain and Ireland. Have we ever asked ourselves 'what is out there'. Or was out there in an earlier time. The oceans are a bigger world hugging the shores than those seas towards the continent. Our sedentary lives seem to be seen to be busy to remain contented to ignore the bigger picture of what really is around us. Does it matter? Is boredom much bigger than the oceans that makes them inconsequential to our lives? Perhaps it is perceived from London that Wales is the furthest west we can go because that is how the Romans did see it then after they landed and condemned the local tribal Britains to excommunication to a land they dubbed as the lands of the foreigners, namely Wales. Small minds and quick solutions serve a practical purpose. Still big oceans do not go away and we still know nothing about an early past and should we.

Ship captain pilots sometimes describe their responsibilities as 99% boredom and 1% terror. Obviously that boredom must be a lot bigger in the oceans. Still something compelling must drive their nature to remain in their jobs on the oceans if boredom is so large. Perhaps the infinite celestial horizons feeds their dreams where the sense of power is endless. They know in the vast space of earth oceans they must learn to respect humility and to follow the rules to the letter because they know they are always only a mistake away from disaster. It becomes like a sacred trust unlike money that holds trust only that is not sacred.

The seas off the coast of Wales are not oceans yet people generally in London might believe that they are and as a result have no idea what oceans are like, unlike the seas off the west coast of Ireland where nature makes a pact with wind and water and with sun and earth and with multiple combinations that shape the local landscape hugging the ocean with its mighty pen of high cliffs and wild white capped waves foaming as in a black and white minstrel show.

If you have never visited these westerly shores there must have been a good reason and I guess that you never knew where the real oceans were and that they were so near you. Now you do know. Perhaps you will stand someday on the beach and look far out into the vast expanse and touch an early past and feel that spirit of early man (homo sapiens) when they first arrived on these shores from Africa. Then that will be a revelation a new explosion and life thereafter becomes a new experience.

You can only blame the Irish Government and their gold gilt senior employees in their administrations for this ignorance who have blinded your quest to discover more because they make something easy much more complicated and expensive. Understanding a sow eating its own farrow can best describe why more Irish people live elsewhere than natives in their native land and soon foreigners will exceed them too.

Why has no academic study been carried out before by the administrations in Ireland to determine the real findings of an earlier language history of a primitive time and why have administration policies succumbed to external demands from locations nearer to Deutsch Post than to the GPO in Dublin? Why does the Irish Government give authority to those that command a kind of ersatz respectability where their predations, illusions and vanities become public policy? Where is their official evidence of findings of an earlier time of the language spoken by a primitive man on the shore of the Isles? These failings of accountability are negligence and abuse of overpaid responsibility and failing to honour a proper code of allegiance with the people on these islands they represent. This Faustian pact of ill-gotten gains and very poor productivity demonstrates a cult like administration that deny the people the root of our words

29

that makes our minds think. The sovereignty of this 'republic of sows' should declare their hands and show transparency and allow the people find their real sovereignty in a world of today that matters.

TINNITUS IN WORDS

Words we speak have an origin. They may not be recent and they may be a very long time ago. Maybe man learned some from animals too. It is difficult to imagine how words first were used and where they came from.

The Irish language did have a substrate language spoken on The Isles prior to the arrival of people from Europe known as The Celts. This evidence has revealed that this language arrived directly by boat from West Africa in an area now known as Senegal and was never part of the language chemistry mixing with other languages from elsewhere in the world prior to arrival on The Isles. Recorded languages only reveal those people that travelled eastwards and along the Nile River. This compilation includes more than 100 words and also 10 words on Ptolemy's map never encrypted before. Historical research from the best official printed books gathered to date acknowledge that there has been no evidence of proof of any ancient words as old and readers are requested to only resort to assumptions. This new evidence in this compendium changes that stalemate and should be studied to learn more about who we are, how we think and why and how these people saw our lands many many many thousands of years earlier.

The effort in locating this new revelation is pale compared to finding paid responsible civil servants of The State to examine these findings and report thereon. This exercise has shown how inept and naïve their policies and lack of them are. This void in our nationalism as a sovereign country and the disrespect shown to our culture can only show to the next generation and emigrants how hopeless we Irish want to remain as a people we once were.

When homo sapiens arrived on the isles of Britain and Ireland there were no other humans, other than a few that landed in Kent, thus there was never any interbreeding between homo sapiens and Neanderthals on the isles. They were pure sapiens what travelled directly from West Africa. Subsequent arrivals on the isles from Europe may have already interbreed, but these arrived no sooner than 10,000 BC and a lot later than pure sapiens. When they arrived they were more muscular and better adapted to cold climates and their cognitive skills more advanced and may have accounted for their supremacy and achievements in replacement of the earlier arrivals directly from Africa.

These homo sapiens cooperated as an ancient archaic tribe that was rooted in common myths that exist only in people's collective imagination. The effigy known as 'Sile na Gig' derives itself directly from their native language, (see compendium) and would have been used to propagate a myth of their time. It appears to have shown a strong heterosexual significance and a source of power to a greater being. This myth bonded their tribe as a unit and formed part of a social order of prominence that they practiced. Feckland (Kerry) was the location that this effigy shows its prominence and would be comparable to present day locations for spiritual practices such as Rome, Mecca, Jerusalem etc.

Their myths were their stories of their own invention that did not exist elsewhere. Their myths manifested between themselves as 'our stories' i.e. 'seanos'. Sile na Gig would undoubtedly have been the earliest evidence of a social belief on the isles and from this they developed their laws and justice, their prejudices and fears and their shamans (file) and sorcerers. Their social practices were 'fictious', 'social constructs' and/or imagined realities. They exerted this force in their world then. Other practice parallel to this was the celebration of 'An Poc' or 'Puck Fair' in Killorglin, Kerry. This annual celebration is currently the oldest gathering in Ireland.

These myths are part of the earliest known evidence of the cognitive revelation in Europe and since then sapiens have thus been living in a dual reality that is objective and imagined. History has proven that the imagined reality became more powerful and modern living depends on its existence in trade, commerce and beliefs.

The following are among those state bodies I contacted and refused for reasons they excused as not within their remit: Dept. of The Gaeltacht, Language Commission, Dept. of The Taoiseach and Dept. of Education.

Other contacts that might be considered arms of The State referred me to people that clearly did not have normal Irish names and might have been raised in Eastern Europe and hold specialised qualifications in a form of linguistics that includes comparing all languages that interacted on the continent at some stage prior to arrival in Ireland. They use a theory test that has no relevance to these findings because these words arrived directly from Africa unblemished from other cultures and makes these findings very unique in the language we claim to be our own.

Various Professors of Irish and ancient Irish refused to examine these words. There actions are a betrayal of who we are and can only add to the farce The State promulgates.

Many reasonable Irish people have seen these findings that include Irish Teachers, Native Irish Speakers and other Irish with a general knowledge of Irish and it made a lot of sense to them.

I did approach Trinity College Dublin and could only reach directly by e-mail a male administrator to the Irish section and no further. At this point I was refused any meeting with anyone with relevant qualifications. Then I was requested to submit findings only by e-mail. After no response and making further enquiries I was told my evidence was useless because it did not conform to a theory law on sound relevant to other languages in Europe. I was refused the identity of who read the evidence and after protesting to demand a meeting in person and provoking them to listen to me I was told to go to a Catholic University.

I subsequently submitted a written complaint to the Department of Education who had originally referred me to them and received no response to date.

CONSPECTUS

'To conclude or be damned' is a theory revealing a seminal part in an ancient language structure, spoken by homo sapiens in the Kingdom of Kerry that was pure, original and direct from Africa. These words in their purity reveal a pattern and a concept that shows a signal that is significant. This theory denounces the existing academic practices in synchronic studies as irrelevant for this purpose.

This theory dismisses the Genesis Myth (11:1-9) for these homo sapiens because it did not apply to those that founded The Kingdom of Kerry because their journey was not the same path used on which the story of mankind is based upon. Their path eclipsed Noah, The Torah, The Bible, and The Koran.

An Enigma.

LANGUAGE IS A CURRENCY

All spoken languages are currencies with value and their price depends how much trust is given to it by the speakers. Like most currencies there is little value back up security such as gold yet some fiat currencies have prime value over others. What makes the difference is the trust that is placed into it by the market. In this case those who speak and or use it.

Sometimes the market is fudged by the government and the demand becomes artificial where regulations force the demand to increase when in fact the real life in the language is negligible. This can be observed by comparing the few number of Irish Speakers with extensive Government Regulations.

Observations show that the official Irish language ignores the root in Gaelic and that what The State promulgates is simply just an official Irish language in the EU. This means just official and just legislation. This is like cloning dolly the sheep or creating a florescent rabbit. The absence of real life blood emaciates the corpse of the language to a metaphor. Imaginary. This cold feeling spreads and life freezes what remains.

Gaelic is the original substrate language that arrived along the west coast of Ireland by boat and this holds the spirit and drive in the life it gives to this maritime nation. Gaelic arrived originally in Kerry and directly from Africa and these words in this compendium are unique in their originality and their precision to connect with a very primitive time in the history of man. No other European language can attest to this because theirs fused with many others many thousands of years later. Gaelic is a pure original.

Interactions with the organs of the State show their exclusion to Gaelic by imposing foreign hypothesis managed by foreigners when it is not relevant. Their failure to recognise the uniqueness of the substrate language and Gaelic and more importantly the absence of government policy to have native qualified professor with this mandate to develop this opportunity bleeds the nation. This can be compared to the ECB in Europe dictating the money needs of the banking requirements of the nation and excluding the Central Bank in Dublin except in this case Gaelic language should belong to the Irish only.

Both by implication of failed government policies the organs of The State including The Irish Language Commission have conspired in creating a sense of an 'assumed consensus' (even in the face of contradictory evidence), alienating dissenting opinions, retarding problems-solving, inhibiting the expression of doubts and suppressing the conception, discussion and action of alternate options. Decision – making becomes skewed in such scenario and can lead to negative results.

Knowing the real ancient origins of your native language promotes the critical thinking and awareness of the people on these islands and their conceptualisation of the outside world. Had we been wiser we may have prevented the Bank Crisis in 2008.

COMPENDIUM OF THE OLDEST WORDS ON THE ISLES OF BRITAIN & IRELAND

- Map of Ireland Deciphered

- Ptolemy's Map of Ireland

- Map

- Irish Politics

- Boats in Ireland

- Map

- Irish Landscape

- Kingdom of Kerry

- Miscellaneous

- GAA Sports

- Irish Family Names

- Muck Ross and Homo Sapiens

PTOLEMY'S MAP OF IRELAND

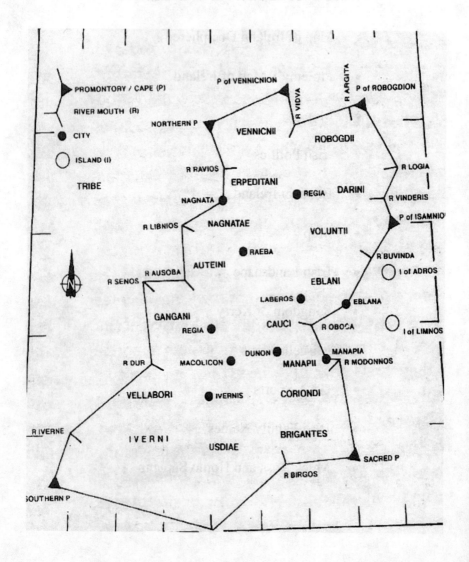

PROMONTORY / CAPE (P)

RIVER MOUTH (R)

CITY

ISLAND (I)

TRIBE

P of VENNICNION

NORTHERN P

VENNICNII

R VIDVA

R ARGITA

P of ROBOGDION

ROBOGDII

R LOGIA

R RAVIOS

ERPEDITANI

REGIA

DARINI

R VINDERIS

NAGNATA

P of ISAMNIO

R LIBNIOS

NAGNATAE

VOLUNTII

RAEBA

AUTEINI

R BUVINDA

I of ADROS

R AUSOBA

R SENOS

EBLANI

LABEROS

EBLANA

GANGANI

CAUCI

R OBOCA

I of LIMNOS

REGIA

R DUR

MACOLICON

DUNON

MANAPIA

MANAPII

R MODONNOS

VELLABORI

IVERNIS

CORIONDI

R IVERNE

IVERNI

USDIAE

BRIGANTES

SACRED P

R BIRGOS

SOUTHERN P

Senos (wolof) = our river (marked on Ptolemy's map of Ireland indicating the Shannon river) Sinn (Gaelic) = our; and (also see Roose (wolof).

The River Shannon and Senegal River both have east/west orientation and are similar.

Gangani (location as shown on Ptolemy's map of Ireland):

This is made up of two words in Wolof;

Gandax (wolof) meaning 'wave'; and

Ganaar (wolof) meaning 'gentle' or 'timid'

Thus the local historical boat 'Gandelow' located further inland on the Shannon River is 'a timid wave boat'. This can be seen by examining how lower the bow of the boat is.

Conclusion: The word Gangani thus is a safe place for local boats. This location has now been identified as the estuary shore lands of New Town Clarina close to Lymericke City.

Eblana (location on Ptolemy's map of Ireland)

This is made of two words in Wolof:

Eb (wolof) meaning 'to load'

Laana (wolof) meaning 'to be open' (expression)

The location on the map indicates that this was south of the river Liffey in Dublin. Thus the meaning is:

'Open place in the docks south of the river Liffey to load'. This would indicate that from earliest times all exports were loaded on the south side.

Eblani (location on Ptolemy's map of Ireland)

This is made of two words in Wolof:

Eebi (wolof) meaning 'to unload'

Laana (wolof) meaning 'to open' (expression)

The location on the map indicates that this was north of the river Liffey in Dublin. Thus the meaning is:

'Open place in the docks north of the river Liffey to unload '. This would indicate that from earliest times all imports were unloaded on the north side.

Nagnatae (location on Ptolemy's map of Ireland)

This is made up of two words in Wolof:

Nag (wolof): this means 'Cow'.

Nata (wolof): this means 'to measure '

The location of this word on Ptolemy's map indicates in the centre of Ireland.

Conclusion: 'Cattle Herd on the rich grasslands',

Robogdi (location on Ptolemy's map of Ireland):

This is made up of two words in Wolof:

Roob (wolof): this means 'to bury'.

Bugga (wolof): this means 'to want'.

The location of this word is at the famous The Giants Causeway.

This word is challenging. Does it mean a raised ground to form a path and or is it the trampling and ramming technique for consolidating also to make a path as the legend tells us. Looking at the basalt rock formations did primitive man perceive that that the rocks were being trampled as they went into the sea to make a raised ground.

Laboros (location on Ptolemy's map of Ireland)

This is made up of two words in Wolof:

Laa (wolof): this means 'place'.

Bari (wolof): this means 'plenty'.

The location on Ptolemy's map indicates in the south central part of Ireland where the rich arable lands predominate for tillage farming.

Menapii (location on Ptolemy's map of Ireland)

Men (wolof): to be able to do something better:

Piis (wolof): piece of material: (see also miscellaneous)

This indicates a place for manufacturing value added products.

Ireland

Original Meanings of Homo Sapien Language in The Kerry Empire

Dangerous Lough

Sarong

Cursed Island

Trampling Rocks

Silver Shine Land

Semi Desert

Fertility Lake (Spawn)

Elbow Lake

Smile

Island of worship

Land of Rabbits

Hole

Safe Islands

Sarong Bracelet

Cattle Herd Country

Importing

Thumb Island

Cattle Insemination

Place to climb

Gaal Boat Harbour

Woman's Vagina

Silver Shine Land

Royal Place

Exporting

Speed Boats

Pond Lake

Roving Farmlands

Safe Place to Land

Pounded

Peaceful Waters

Thigh

Island of Boats

Our River

Fast Goat Splashes

Place of Manufacturing

Fishing Boats

Dangerous Rocks

Lamb Mountains

White Man Arrives

Pock Fair

Place of Information

Irish Dancing

Spiritual Capital

Quiet Water Lake

Baby Splash Boats

Fertility Worship Center

Poiteen Making

Finger

Safe Place For Boats

Difficult Uneconomic Land

IRISH POLITICS

Firdu (wolof) - means 'Tribe'

Fir (gaelic) = men

Fianna (gaelic) = warriors

Today the following are among the largest parties in Irish Politics:

Fianna Fáil, Fianna Gael and Sinn Féin

Sen (wolof) – means 'our'

Today the Senate in Ireland known as the Seanad is 'our voice'.

Irish House of Commons

Da-jaloo (wolof) means to gather together; and

Da-jee (wolof) means to meet with.

Today the ' Dáil' is the Irish House of Commons as a place to meet

Boats in Ireland

Gaal (wolof) means a 'large boat to carry people or folk'. It is made up of two words in Wolof as follows:

Gaa (wolof) means people or folks; and

Laa (wolof) means bed.

Thus it was seen as a large folk bed that floats on the ocean as in a sea version of a Volkswagen.

This was the original large manual sea boat with a lift up in its bow to ride the ocean waves and was used to travel the long distance to Ireland. It would have held more than twenty people. This majestic vehicle was in its time the greatest technology made by ancient man and finally made its home on the Shannon Estuary.

In the centre of Lymericke city the present Kings Island has had an earlier older name: Inis an Ghaill Duibh that has caused confusion to its origins. We can now conclude that this means the island of the Black Gals.

(See also chapter on Irish Family Names)

Currach (wolof) means a baby splash boat.

This gave us the present boat along the Irish shoreline known as the Currach. The name from Wolof is liken to a young goat who piddles all over the place and wets everything. The smell of salt in their urine excites them wild jumping as in sea splashes and rapid splashes. Its purpose was to make a smaller version of the Gaal to sail into the numerous shorelines along the coast after arrival and settlement. This boat had the ability to manoeuvre between shorter distances. The canvas of the original boats was made from goat's skin.

Cas (wolof)

This means a sea fishing boat with lines. Cashin boats are found near the mouth of the Shannon Estuary and are a variation of the Currach.

Ooor (wolof) This means 'to keep fast' or 'speed'.

Hooker boat is the fast version of the Currach because it has raised sails to give it speed.

This word is pronounced uuuuuuuukr. Its pronunciation espouses the thrill of speed or the fear of it. There is no 'h' in the Wolof alphabet. This word is also a very rare example that demonstrates the intimate connection between primitive man and the monkey. It has been studied and proven from professional research that the monkey gives out this particular sound when they are been attacked by an Eagle. To understand this deeper this fine bird of prey has far distant precise eyesight and when attacking it does so with enormous speed. (see graph) This word would be a precursor to the expression 'cute hoor'.

Kot (wolof) This means 'alone'.

In Ireland Cot boats are found in some of our southern smaller inland rivers that only hold one person. It is a version of a small canoe as we know them today. This boat is a tradition along the Abbey River (Lymericke)

Homo Sapiens on boat island, Curraghgower, Lymericke

Cittie of Lymericke

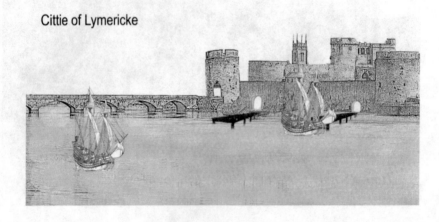

Cittie of Lymericke

Lymericke today

IRISH LANDSCAPE

Rivers & Seas:

Senos (wolof): This means 'Our River'. (See Ptolmey's Map) (See Roose (wolof))

We can deduce why it was called this name because these primitive people once lived along the Senegal River and this river is similar to the Shannon Estuary that it flows from west to east direction with similar size and glory. You will note that 'gal' is at the end of this word Senegal and that indicates the nature of boats in their river too.

Deelu (wolof): This means 'dead water'.

The Deel River is a tributary of the Shannon and it is situated in quiet waters for their boats to harbour.

Mag (wolof): This means an older sibling/cousin.

The Maigue River is also a nearby tributary to the Deel River.

Luppa (wolof) This means 'a thigh' as in a leg. (See Graph)

Loop Head peninsula at the mouth of the Shannon is in the shape of a thigh.

Feelit (wolof) This means 'a splinter' (See Graph Map)

Feale River is shaped like a splinter river with many tributaries at the mouth of the Shannon Estuary.

Surga (wolof) This means 'roving farmlands'.

Suir River in County Tipperary passes through some of the most fertile farm land in Ireland known as the Golden Vale and rich in tillage.

Déeg (wolof) This means 'a pond'.

Loch Derg on the Shannon is one of the largest inland lakes in Ireland. Also Lok (wolof) means Loch (Gaelic) and Lough.

Fer (wolof) This means low tide or tidal river.

Fergus River is a tidal river tributary on the Shannon.

Foyle (wolof) This means Dangerous / Risk.

Carrig Foyle along the Shannon Estuary would mean dangerous rocks as would Loch Foyle in Donegal: Dangerous Lough.

Ees Kees (wolof) These are two words:

Ees (wolof) meaning 'new'

Kees (wolof) meaning 'safe place'

Askeaton town along the Shannon Estuary is thus a new safe place to keep the boats in harbour. Also Inis Kea, North and South islands off the west coast.

Ees Deelu (wolof) These are two words:

Ees (wolof) meaning 'new'

Deelu (wolof) meaning 'dead water'

Asdee a village in Kerry along the Shannon Estuary is thus a safe place in quiet waters to harbour the boats.

Dal Kees (wolof) This means a 'safe place to meet'.

Dalkey (Irish Town south of Dublin along the sea coast. The English believed that when Napoleon was in power in France that the then uninhabited area around Dalkey was too easy for ships to arrive so they began building their watch out fortresses in that area thus the now famous Martello Tower as featured in James Joyce novels became part of that.

Caapa (wolof) This means 'vagina'.

Primitive man originally spoke a simple language and often their expressions manifested themselves into body parts. In Ireland the word Cappagh can be often found in many place names in the country with often meaning small boat harbours.

Lef (wolof) This means 'Vagina'. (See Map)

Primitive man realised that the location where Dublin now lies held a prominent location to trade and had studied the shape of the bay intimately. The Liffey River flows into this bay.

Currach (wolof) This means baby splashes.

Curragh Gabhair (Curragower) Water Falls in Lymericke are famous water falls known as the baby goats falls. The image of these beautiful fast water falls conjures baby goats going crazy when either pees on each other. The salt in the pee excites all goats and to want to eat wherever the pee lies. The wild splashes in the falls when the tide is out is the image of the pee the goats make when a lot are together.

Gaaw (wolof) This means quick and swiftly. Thus Currach Gaaw is the original name of the now Curragower (Falls).

Gaal (wolof) This means boat.

We have already read this meaning to be the name of the first boat to arrive on our shores. Many place names have taken their names from this boat. These include:

Galway – gailimh (gaelic)

Dun Gaal (wolof) This means island of the Gaal boats. Donegal is the location in Ireland. It is also strange that there is a Donegal point on the coastline of Co. Clare called Donegal Pt. The name

Donegal has origins in Kerry and Clare too and not always County Donegal.

Galey River Kerry and the Galey Bay near the source of the Shannon River.

Weex (wolof) This means 'white'.

Wexford is located on the most south eastern coast of Ireland at that part closest to the Continent. This seems to indicate that primitive Black Man in Ireland first saw the arrival of White man from the Continent.

Tuur (wolof) This means 'to spill'/'to pour'.

Turlough (Hiberno Irish) is a lake on a mountain. Its image is like water that was poured into an enclosed area.

Ree (wolof) This means 'to smile' or 'to laugh'.

Lough Ree has the shape of a smile. (see graphs)

Naaw (wolof) This means 'semi desert' or 'open field'.

Lough Neagh is the largest inland lake in Ireland covering a semi desert of sand. Currently Lord Shaftsbury owns the rights to extract sand for supply.

Bayaal (wolof) Open Space

Béal – gaelic mouth

Ness (wolof) This means 'flicker' (see family name Shaughnessy).

Lough Ness in Scotland got its name from the flicker of the Northern Lights.

Mallam (wolof) This is a garment used to wrap around the waist. (serong)

Malahide – near Dublin. This large bay has a tiny entrance.

Also Malin in Donegal.

Lam (wolof) A bracelet /bangle.

Lambay Island near Dublin.

Concó (wolof) – This means elbow.

Lough Conn (Mayo) is in the shape of an elbow.

Roose (wolof) – This means water.

Rosslare, Rosses Point, New Ross, Muck Ross (Killarney), Rosmuc ,Rosscarbery are all places beside water.

Mucca (wolof) – This means quiet.

Muck Ross (Killarney) is a famous quiet lake.

Tuura (wolof) This means 'Moon'.

The Hill of Tara has the distinction of been shaped like a Moon Hill for a place of ancient worship.

Other Landscapes:

Connaught This means the land of rabbits.

Ów (wolof) A place to climb

Howth – near Dublin

Mis (wolof) This means lamb.

Slieve Mish in Kerry

Torex (wolof) This means a cursed place to suffer.

Tory Island – Donegal

Baaraam (wolof) This means 'finger' or 'toe'.

Inish Bara Island in Co. Galway has the shape of a toe/thumb.

Beara Penninsula has the shape of a finger.

Bón Bónna (wolof) This means a 'hole'.

Brú na Bóinne (Gaelic) – Megalithic site. This word is the precursor for the Boyne River.

Tuur (n)(wolof) This means a shrine, idol, spirit.

There are two Inish Turk islands off the coast of Mayo and in the middle of Lough Ree. Kanturk, Co. Cork is a place of animal worship.

Mooka (wolof) This means to be well pounded.

This refers to the Cliffs of Moher.

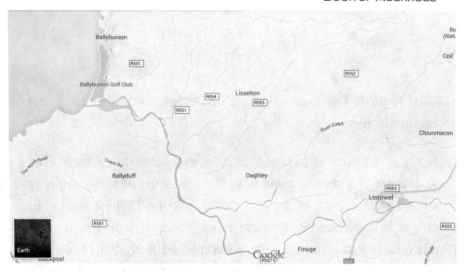

Feelit (wolof) – Splinter – Feale River

Lef (wolof) – Vagina – Dublin Bay (Liffey River)

59

KINGDOM OF KERRY

Kéri (wolof) This means a place of struggle both physically and economically.

Kerry is that part of Ireland that is located nearest to Africa. This wolof meaning does explain what the landscape of Kerry really is and it is that part of Ireland that holds the highest mountain ranges in the country. Tourism is its principal industry. It is in this county that primitive man has continued to show its blueprint and its original home where its own empire did spread throughout the island and elsewhere. Every Kerry man has told the world that they come from the Kingdom of Kerry and this is a state of mind passed down to every generation yet there has been no record of a Kerry Empire before now and the information in this compendium will change that forever.

Mokk Pooc (wolof) This means 'a good wife'.

Maith Poch (Gaelic) This means a 'good goat'.

Bulo (wolof) This means 'to hit with ones fist'.

Búla (Gaelic) This means 'to hit with ones fist'.

In South Kerry every year the annual Poc Fair is celebrated where a certain eligible wild goat is captured in the high mountains and paraded through the town of Kilorglin. It is claimed that this is an ancient practice in Kerry. To date they do not know how or why it started. This can now be explained.

Along the Senegal River there is a similar annual celebration by the Lebou people that has been there also since ancient times. This is known as the Ndeup Rituals. The horns of their goats grow sideways from the Goat's head. The Kerry goat grows his horns upwards and back. Primitive man when first they saw these goats in Kerry they imagined ' a good wife with her fists up to fight'. Thus the gaelic name 'Maith Poc ag buile' or in wolof 'Mokk pooc ag bulo'. (see GAA Sports (Gaelic))

Kéru Buur (wolof) This means' Royal Household'.

Kerry Gold is a commercial name coined by a famous successful Irish man who also lived in the then catchment area of the extended Kingdom of Kerry (Castlemartin).

It is interesting that primitive man created a Royal Household in Kerry and that this mind-set continues today. Gold was used in Kerry to support this Kingdom. So where did it come from?

Baaraam (wolof) This means 'finger' or 'toe'.

Beara Peninsula is in the shape of a finger'.

Buur (wolof) This means 'royal'

Ruux (wolof) This means spiritual soul.

Brian BORÚ can now mean Brian the King of Soul/Spiritual King. It must be noted even though Brian Ború was seated in Lymericke city his kingdom included Kerry. Also the descendants of Brian built a Cathedral in Lymericke on Kings Island that was completed before the Notre Dame in Paris that also was built on an island.

Fii (wolof) This means 'to sow'.

Fis (gaelic) This means information. It compares the learning with sowing and where growth follows.

Fexa (wolof) This means 'to seek a way, try, attempt, and manage'.

In Kerry the renowned commercial company Fexco is a world leader in this field.

Ag Renka (wolof) This means 'doing crooked legs '.

Ag Rince (Gaelic) This means Irish Dancing

Fola (wolof) This means 'to go through you'.

Fola (Gaelic) This means 'blood'.

Deoch Fhola (gaelic) means bad blood = Dracula.

Lal (wolof) This means 'bed'.

Leaba (Gaelic) means 'bed'.

Oor (wolof) (pronounced hoor) This means 'Gold'.

In Kerry a compliment is given to someone when they are described as a 'cute hoor'. This denotes that the person is a winner, got away with it no matter how they did it and it won't be questioned: a fast thing, a momentary title, and accolade.

'Sile na Gig' (see compendium) This is an ancient myth practiced mainly in Kerry.

*Sheelagh na Gig
Artist: Suzanne Mortell*

Roose (wolof) – This means water.

Rosslare, Rosses Point, New Ross, Muck Ross (Killarney), Rosscarbery are all places beside water.

(See Seanos (wolof) – Our River)

Mucca (wolof) – This means quiet.

Muck Ross (Killarney) is a famous quiet lake.

From the families of religious priests and worshipers in Kerry – Sugrues – **Sukka**(wolof) – to kneel/genuflect and **Ruux**(wolof) – soul

Concó (wolof) – This means elbow.

Lough Conn (Mayo) is in the shape of an elbow.

Mis (wolof) - This means lamb / quiet place.

Slieve Mish in Kerry

Torup (wolof) - Too, very and how! (Emphasises a previous judgement)

Torup – Is she pretty!

Torc Falls, Killarney

GAA Sports

See page 71

MISCELLANEOUS

Dal (wolof) This means 'land'.

Dal Riada/Dal Glas (ancient Irish kingdoms)

Teer (wolof) This means 'land'; this land is land on the shoreline only.

Tír (Gaelic) This means 'land'.

In Wolof there are different words for land and their location determine what word is used. Land can be shoreline, inland, cultivation and fishing.

Lír (wolof) This means 'infants'.

Lír (Gaelic) means 'infants'. The Children of Lir.

Naam (wolof) This means 'name'

Anaim (Gaelic) means 'name'.

Olu (wolof) This means 'trust'

Olamh (Gaelic) means professor. Someone to trust with information.

Potit (wolof) This means 'wash water'.

Potín (Gaelic) alcohol made from wash water.

Ag Riddi (wolof) This means 'running fast'.

Ag Rith (Gaelic) means running fast.

Taxa (wolof) This means 'to stick'. (See separate chapter)

Taxation means a demand to pay.

Can (wolof) This means 'to be stucked'. (See separate chapter)

Cáin (Gaelic) means taxation as per Irish Finance Acts.

Sore Can (wolof) This means far and away from being stucked.

Saor Ó Cáin (Gaelic) means 'free from tax'.

Oom (wolof) This means 'to be abundant'.

Ogham (Gaelic) means information written on stone.

Em Raam (wolof) This means 'to fit by crawling slowly together'.

Imram (old Gaelic) means 'to make a rhythm of two ideas.

Findi Fay (wolof) This means 'to blacken and throw oneself'

Fith Fath (old Gaelic) means the 'secret of shape shifting to appear invisible '.

Anam (wolof) This means 'soul'.

Anam (Gaelic) means 'soul'.

Ag (wolof) This means 'and/with '

Agus/ag (Gaelic) means and/with.

Fanaan (wolof) This means 'stay'.

Fan anseo (Gaelic) stay (here).

Coleen (wolof) This means 'style appearance'.

Cailín (Gaelic) means 'girl'.

Colin (wolof) This means a 'name for a man with style and appearance'.

Colin is an Irish name. Also Mountcollins (town) near the Shannon Estuary.

Taa (wolof) = This means 'to accept'.

Tá (Gaelic) = Yes

Cam (wolof) Interjection used to express disgust about or filth.

Family name 'Cambell'. ie. Cam Béal – Crooked Mouth

Sex (wolof) This means 'to suck'.

Yefu say-saay (wolof) This means sex in Wolof only.

It is presumed that like taxation the word sex was originally used in Kerry before it did spread throughout the isles of Britain and Ireland.

Seela (wolof) This means 'crevice – vagina in this case' as in 'Síla na Gig'.

Gi (wolof) This means 'the, his and her'– Síle na Gig (a figurative carving of a woman displaying her vulva) – This is found in many places in Ireland and its purpose has been unknown to now examples can be found in the Round Tower in Rattoo in Kerry and a replica in the museum in Tralee.

Na (wolof) This means 'from, through'

Síle na Gig means her vagina.

Fec (wolof) This means to make a big hole in it.

Fec (Gaelic) and Feck used in Ireland only as in Hiberno English to mean as 'a euphemistic substitute for fuck'.

Ban (Wolof) This means 'refuse'.

Jaxxal (Wolof) This means 'to doubt'.

Banjax (Anglo Irish) – broken, incapacitated.

Aron (Wolof) This means 'silver'.

There are a few Aran Islands off the coast of Ireland and Scotland. This would indicate that on the arrival of primitive man they saw from the sea in their boats the sparkle of the sun on the limestone landscape of these islands and called them 'silver'.

Marabu (Wolof) This means 'a person that has gone to the spirits.

Marbh (Gaelic) means a dead person.

Dugga (Wolof) This means 'to enter'.

Duganna (Gaelic) means 'harbour'.

Dun (Wolof) This means 'an island'.

Many places in Ireland are called Dun… or Don…It is to assume that primitive man originally thought they were landing on an island initially before they carried out a full survey of that area. Donegal is a large county in the North-West of Ireland

Ruux (v) (wolof) This means to investigate. (something secret)

Rún (n) (Gaelic) This means 'secret'

Deédeét (wolof) This means 'no'

In Kerry, when a person refuses demands by someone else in public place the wave their hands and say 'daye dayet'. There is no equivalent in Irish/Gaelic or English.

Ee (wolof) This means to call someone's attention to wake up.

Geten (wolof) This means to bother, annoy, pester.

Eegit (This is Hiberno Irish) This means 'Idiot'

Piis (wolof) This means to wink or look through the corner of your eye.

'Taking the piss out of me' is a common expression in Cork/Kerry

Tali (wolof) This means outside ground.

Talaimh (Gaelic) this means outside ground.

GAA SPORTS (GAELIC)

Cammoon (wolof) This means 'left side'/'left hand extension when visible'.

Camán (Gaelic) = Hurley used in Gaelic Games

Camóg (Gaelic) = Hurley used in Gaelic Games. (smaller)

Camógaíocht (Gaelic) = Hurley used by ladies.

This is held upper with left hand where the weight rest and the right hand balances the hurley.

Caadi – Caadi (wolof) This means to roll on the ground.

Caid (Gaelic) This is a ball used to play hurling in Kerry and nearby regions. (Old Gaelic).

Mokk Pooc ag Bulo (wolof) This means a fighting woman with raised fist.

Maith Poc ag Bula (Gaelic) This is an expression for a good ball passing on the playing pitch.

Gaelic is in essence the sports of the earliest boat people that arrived on the Isles of Britain and Ireland and has its original meaning in the name of a boat.

Gaelic was the substrate language to sports on the Isles of Britain and Ireland.

Irish Family Names

Many western seashore Irish Family names are derived from Wolof as follows:

From the **Gaal** Boats:

Gallaghers, Garveys, Galligans, Gallivans, etc

From the Fishermen: **Mool** (Wolof)

Mulligans, Mullallys, Molloys, Mullherns etc

From the land husbandry: **Laal** (Wolof)

Lallys, Mullallys etc.

From the Islands **Dun** (Wolof) 'islands'

Donnells, Dunphys etc

From the land of cattle breeders: **Teer** (Wolof) and **Nagnatae** (Ptolemy's Map)

Tiernan, Tearnan

From the land of fertility worshipers: **Seela** (wolof)

Shea, O'Shea, Shee, Sheedy, Sheehan, Sheahan, Sheehy

From the land of Enemy Families (Vikings) - The Shannon Estuary: **Noon** (wolof)

Noonan/Noons/Nunan – This family name was given to Vikings that arrived along the estuary.

From the inland River Shannon, along the Lymericke North Tipperary side, were the friendly, smiling, laughing families: **Ree**(wolof) – Smile (see Map of Ireland - Lough Ree in the shape of a smile)

Ryan (pronounced 'reen' in Gaelic) – Originally settled along the banks of the River Shannon

From the land of Our River Guards (Shannon Estuary – Lymericke): **Sen**(wolof) 'our', and **Ness**(wolof) ' flicker'.

These families along the shore lit fires on arrival of enemies to warn others further inland.

Shaughnessy

From the families of religious priests and worshipers in Kerry – Sugrues – **Sukka**(wolof) – to kneel/genuflect and **Ruux**(wolof) - soul

It had to be normal that these primitive men would give names to places to indicate their then superior technology namely the Gaal Boat i.e. Galway, Donegal and Kings Island in Lymericke city. Sometimes the original names sink beyond recognition over subsequent time. I believe that understanding the trend at that time the town Dingle was also a version of Donegal to harbour their boats. The reason its name has changed so much has been due to the influence of the Vikings to make the name sound Norse. That is why the name Dingle persists today.

Trends do give insights and this previously unknown Kerry Empire held its original sway over Kerry Limerick and Clare before advancing further. The Shannon Estuary was originally its only known world then.

Muckross & Homo Sapiens

TRENDS

Trends by definition show a direction and a mind-set that may assist the authentication of what is being presented. The following evidence adds to the periphery of thoughts shown in this compendium and its tautology should make it meaningful.

Boats:

There are six types of ancient boats identified in Wolof that can be attributed to being Irish by nature by their very existence and names. All come from ancient Gaelic words and now they have been retrieved. These are Gaal, Currach, Hooker, Cashin, Gandelow and the Cot.

In addition the importance of present day Kings Island in the centre of Limerick has a new meaning as a place for the custodian of the Gaal boats as in its Gaelic meaning 'Inis na Geal Dubh'. This now brings into focus the forgotten underwater smooth razor shaped dark ancient rock surfaces jutting from the foot of the walls of the castle that can only be seen when the tide is really out. These are remnants of primitive infrastructure for holding boats and even today indicates a pattern of ancient mooring in its day, now all forgotten and buried and unscripted on any current parchment or paper; and (See Graph).

Body Parts:

Early man used languages of body parts to express intentions of objects and conversation. From the compendium the following include:

		Wolof:
Good Fighting woman	Maith poch ag buile	Mokk pooc ag bulo
Large Vagina	Dublin Harbour	Liffe (Liffey)
Thigh of Leg	Loop Head	Luppa
Trampling Feet	Giant's Causeway (Ptolemy's map)	Robogdi
Sex	T Suck	Sex
Vagina	Síle Na Gig	Gi/Seela/na
Blood	To go through	Fola
Baby pissing/plash boat	Currach	Currach
Small harbour (small vagina)	Capagh	Caapa

(Had Dublin not have had a river the bay might have been called 'capagh')

Wild young goats pissing on the rocks (When the tide is out)	Curragh gabhair falls	Currach Gaaw (Limerick)
Mouth of River	Béal	Bayaal
Elbow	Lough Conn	Concó

		Wolof:
Toe	Inish Bara	Baaraam
Finger	Beara Penninsula	Baaraam
To be a pest	-	Piis
Outside Ground	Talaimh	Tali

Lands:

Inland Property	Dal	Dal
Shore land	Tír	Teer
Fishing Land	Mul	Mool
Roving Farm Lands	Suir River	Surga (Ptolemy's map)
Outside Grounds	Talaimh	Tali
Royal Land	Burren	Buur

Fiscal:

Taxation	Taxation	Taxa
Taxation	Cáin	Can
Free of Tax	Saor ó Cáin	Sore Can

Gold & Silver:

Gold	High King BrianBorú	Buur
Kerry Gold	Kerry Gold	Kéru Buur
	Plenty/Beara Peninsula	Bari
		(Ptolemy's map)
Aran Islands	Aran	Indicates
(there are a few)		sparkling land to
		see from the boat
		in the ocean as a
		result of their
		limestone rock
		causing the sun
		light reflection
		Aron (Wolof)
		silver

Letter 'H':

The Irish alphabet doesn't contain the letter 'H' even though it appears constantly in modern Irish spelling. The 'H' is used to denote a special effect called lenition - - which is really a fancy way of talking about aspiration of consonants.

The 'H' is used in modern Irish spelling – in older Irish (called Ogham script, as in Wolof: Oom 'meaning to be abundant '), the same effect was noted putting a dot,'séimhiú'. As you can imagine, writing with all sorts of lines and dots and acutes sporting about with the letters got pretty confusing to read. Hence, they introduced the convention of using 'H' to show aspiration (lenition) in written Irish.

In Wolof the letter 'H' is also absent and does not appear. Their spelling of the Hooker boat is thus: Ooor. The repetition of the o's gives the aspiration as the séimhú did in old Irish.

Letter 'V'

Both the Irish/Gaelic and wolof language alphabet do not have the letter 'v'.

Vowels:

The earliest Gaelic language, from homo sapiens, was simple and their words short. All words began or were followed by a vowel only.

Family Names:

As per the compendium the names revealed are all known to be West of Ireland names and with association to coastal lands and fishing.

GAA Sports (Gaelic)

Cammoon (wolof) This means 'left side'/'left hand extension when visible'.

Camán (Gaelic) = Hurley used in Gaelic Games

This is held upper with left hand where the weight rest and the right hand balances the hurley.

Caadi – Caadi (Wolof) This means to role on the ground.

Cad (Gaelic) This is a ball used to play hurling (Gaelic).

Mokk Pooc ag Bulo(wolof) This means a fighting woman with raised fist.

Maith Poc ag Bula(Gaelic) This is an expression for a good ball passing on the playing pitch.

Deciphering the Speed Graph

We are all animals of the Earth and we co-exist in our own ways. Primitive man when hunting knew how 'to listen' and did this; and... 'Silent'. It is interesting that both words contain the same letters. Animal sounds gave coded messages to one another and the hunter honed his skill mastering their intentions so he could prey on them for a home cooked meal or be eaten raw. The instinct of the hunter man was so strong because he had to learn to survive to exist even in a bloodied way because that is what animals do too. Everyone is competing to survive.

It is necessary to insist to conclude in this chapter because in the face of adversity tears away from us all but the things that cannot be torn, so that afterwards we can see ourselves as we really are and not merely as we might like to be. It is like knowing how much we are worth by finding what we are wearing, if any, when the tide goes out. Understood as culturally bankrupt.

Before continuing, let's not conclude that the word 'hooker' means; a prostitute.

The lore about "fighting Capt. John Hooker" in the American Civil War is partially true when he allowed his men to loosen their morals with strange women. He might not be the progenitor of the term 'hooker', but certainly helped it become more widely known.

This conclusion is more serious and for a different reason. The monkey is the progenitor of the first word 'hooker' and as in 'hooker boat' found off the west coast of Ireland. This ancient boat has sails. This chapter may be the only explanation ever given to date how man learned his words from a monkey and then applied them.

Science has proven that Monkeys on the west coast of Africa give out a sound that resonates with 'hooker' and can be spelt in various ways and all sounding similar depending on dialects. This unique sound captured on recording is heard when a crown eagle in flight is seen and is used to indicate speed 'to escape' and 'pending sudden arrival' of this bird of prey to attack other monkeys. It denotes 'speed'. Eagles identify thermal columns rising from the ground, spread their giant wings and allow the hot air to lift them upwards.

The graph attempts to demonstrate the initial perception of the monkey when making sight of this bird to its 'wing span' and how this same idea is also used by man when he made the boat sails of the hooker. Man is seen beside the monkey listening and silent. The hooker boat is a modification of the Curragh boat, a word, that also is from Africa as per the compendium. Mechanical designers have continued to use the wing span of an eagle when designing modern jet fighters. Someday a new modern jet fighter plane will share this appellation.

From the middle of the Jungle in Africa to the west coast of Ireland this word has travelled by man via monkey from an ancient time and is still relevant today. So has its idea traversed the Atlantic showing the influence this inception has done to contribute to man's quest to create more speed in flight even to another world!

84

It is interesting to note that primitive man on the islands of Britain and Ireland had various words (see compendium) for different designations of territorial boundaries that survive in 'Old Irish Gaelic' only, having been lost to the famine period since and deleted in present Irish. Animals too use sounds to share important information about various boundaries and primitive man followed their practice into spoken language. This original bench mark indicates how in present day Irish language the rule of business law has subsumed below the standard code of monkey language level and the Irish banking crisis bears this out. The States policy to allow the departure of Gaelic from its natural root source will allow happen a demise of the true language it originally was and subscribe to its extermination in due course.

Finally, human song was the precursor to spoken language and monkey sounds was the precursor to human song. The traditional Irish singing sean-nos (without music) should now appeal to more than a discerning few.

Research in science demonstrates how successful information is gathered to decipher about monkey language spoken between themselves but has failed to initiate how man in an older time was able to use what they had learned from monkey sounds and being able to apply it in any human language. I believe that Gaelic as in ancient Irish is fortunate and holds the code to exploring more and in good time its importance will finally be recognised. This substantiates the claim to conclude in this presentation. Comparing the words in this compendium with Indo European languages as demanded by pure linguists would best be served with the monkeys who will show you how to speak Gaelic.

Perhaps the Monkey Song resonate everything 'I Want to be like you'.

Speed (The synchronisation between animal language, Gaelic and the American Eagle)

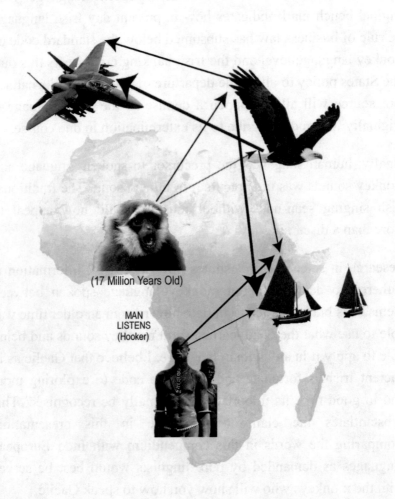

(17 Million Years Old)

MAN
LISTENS
(Hooker)

DECIPHERING THE PAINTING

This original painting was given to me by a lady who received it from her late aunt who lived in County Limerick. This lady is a qualified chartered accountant.

This painting could be an image of what it was once like in Kerry in a swamp lake surrounded by forests and when primitive man hunted in their boats then. It conjures a moment in time so old and so real and what it shows matters a lot more today than meets the eye.

There are two men in this boat and one is standing holding a bow and arrow directing it at a wild deer to kill. The hunter is present in front of the intended victim. With a successful aim the deer will be dead meat. This is what one of the words in the Irish Finance Acts means 'taxation' – 'to stick' - to issue a demand for a tax liability and when you receive it you must pay no matter.

Now I want you to look carefully at the other hunter in the boat who is sitting and rowing only. This is what he normally does when he is hunting in a team. However before he started his day work he had earlier gone elsewhere in the forest 'to set a trap' so as to catch his victim and later the following day return to make his claim and take it home. The process of trapping does not require the presence of the hunter.

Normally during the day an animal is caught in the trap and usually remains alive and cannot escape. As there is no hunter around the animal calls for assistance to escape or to be freed and if and when another animal is passing they might come to the rescue and release the trapped animal. Usually other animals are sympathetic and make great efforts to assist the victim escape. Remember the victim calls the passer by and no hunter was present. This is the interpretation of the word 'Cáin' 'to be stucked' or 'to be trapped'. Always in these cases the process of 'appeal' is used in the Irish Finance Acts and the appeal commissioner is ONLY appointed by the Minister not by the taxpayer.

The findings in this book refute the Ministers interpretation that both words mean the same when in fact they are different.

If a taxpayer is caught in a trap he would like to be able to appoint his own appeal commissioner and not have to use a stranger appointed by the Minister. This is a choice the Irish Taxpayer does have under the interpretations of these substrate words and should be allowed to exercise either of them in a way that suits them. The Minister does not know his Irish, or should it be Gaelic. It can be seen that the primitive Hunter was humane to his animals while the Minister for Finance is inhumane to his fellow human beings. This is Swamp Law for enemies.

The message of primitive man can be taken also to mean 'bank ombudsman' and that the home mortgage holder be allowed to appoint their own ombudsman and not to be at the mercy of The Minister and the Banks.

It is important that from the revelation of these coded words The Minister should not try to stymie the existing wording of the tax law and should transparently inform the electorate in advance his intentions if he decides to change it and not scupper the taxpayer's opportunity by stealth.

Historical Background

The findings from the words discovered reveal that the first people on 'the isles' were black and arrived in boats from Africa. They were hunters, boat builders and fishermen and followed the Puffin bird at sea. They made their kingdom in Kerry and their capital in Lymericke and their homeland stretched all along the Shannon Estuary. They gave the original name to Kings Island in the heart of the city to be 'the island of the gaal boats' or 'boat island' and the local waterfall to be known as the goats splashes'.

They built various designs of boats and these are still being used today. Wood was their technology, tool and weapon and they were masters at using it. Their language was primitive and their words few. Many places took names from body parts and locations to keep their boats. These words are still used today. They travelled all over the island of Ireland and Britain and this is evident from their name given to the Giant Causway marked on Ptolemy's map of Ireland showing it to be Robogdii. They reached the end of the Shannon Estuary and gave names along the way, including Lough Sheelin. (Fertility lake for spawning fish)

They saw their first white man in Wexford and indicated that with reference to the native word Weex meaning 'white. They built a settlement near Lymericke which was called Gangani as indicated on Ptolemy's map.

They formed their own different tribes in good time and took names from their skills as boat builders, fishermen or men from the land and these names continue to flourish today. The West was their origin and their settlements remained strongest there. They brought Irish Dancing and their music to Ireland.

They built their own rock markings as they had done in Senegal. Many of these were upright stones near rivers that eventually formed a Grid System in Ireland and Britain. Some of these stones became marked eventually and known as Ogham (Ooom) stones and predominant in the west of Ireland along the coast. This was the only evidence of their written language.

They had no names for the days of weeks, the months or years. Eventually they maintained cattle herds. Their nomadic life as hunters and gatherers continued in Ireland as it had been in Africa initially. Horses did not form part of their lifestyle and wood remained their only primary technology, tool and weapon. Stone was added subsequently. They were good hunters in the wooded countryside and practiced the art of shape shifting so to catch their prey.

They did not develop a written language and their laws were by word of mount within their tribes. They were spiritual and called their leaders Ború meaning king of soul. They were independent minded and did not form any larger community preferring instead to be rebel minded and feel free in spirit.

They differentiated lands between those that were coastal, for fishermen and inland and gave each a separate word.

They initiated into both languages English and Gaelic the words for Sex, Taxation, Irish Dancing and Poteen. Their language was also a substrate language to English

'THE ISLES' - IRELAND & BRITAIN

Historians like Economist never agree between themselves and the evaluation in this conclusion will invite other opinions. This is part of the purpose to conclude in this book.

Conventional history reveals that there was a substrate language spoken on 'the isle' but are unsure from where or how it arrived. In fact the truth of all their evaluations cannot be tested. Their conventional belief has been that all languages spoken in Europe arrived there via the Nile River or in political correctness ' Indo European'. This fundamentally is their bane.

Due to time constraints, proofs have been confined to the island of Ireland when proving place names derived from The West Atlantic Branch of the Niger Language. These names can also be found in Britain and there is another 'Gangani' in Wales and Ness in Scotland. . That subject is for another time to read.

There is a difference between speaking Gaelic, Celtic and Irish. Nobody seems to have bothered to elucidate on this distinction. And it is significant.

Gaelic was the first language spoken on 'the isle' and that arrived from Wolof tribe who originated from along the Senegalese river. It derived its name from the Gaal boat. The Celts spoke a Celtic language prior to their arrival in 'the isle' from the continent and subsequently Gaelic became absorbed as a substrate and this Creole became commonly referred to as Gaelic. Thus the Celts influenced the direction of this new partnership thereafter because theirs was more sophisticated and structure to absorb and adapt.

The description of Irish as a language was invented at the same time as the Napoleon Code decided by France to centralise the lingua fracas of French of 'Les Isles' in Paris as the national standard for all of France. Like the Ecole Nationale Administrif (ENA) the Irish Bureaucrats and Government agencies massaged Gaelic and invented Irish places names and other words where meanings were not known before. Many of these are fabrications including Luimneach for the city of Lymericke. The Danes gave the city its rightful name from Danish (Lym Ria) meaning a 'dugout river' aptly what the Shannon Estuary actually is. Even Cromwell & Sarsfield, formers foe and friend respectively, rightfully recognised this name. The letter 'e' was added to mean 'and' as in Latin 'et'. Another word that remains commonly misunderstood is 'seanos'. This word is one of the oldest words from Africa and means 'our story/river'. Water is the symbol of feelings and memories of things past. Because of some mishap in recent colonial history this word mistakenly been understood to be 'old story'. Wars can cause changes in these subsequent meanings.

At this point it is important that we ask ourselves what comprises the Irish spoken today. To understand that we must first ask who were The Celts.

In summary they were a bonding of two tribes in Babylonia, one was peaceful and the other warriors. They were known as the Summarians and the Scythians. The Celts crossed Europe and brought with them their deep knowledge of Astrology and Equestrian skills and much of their words from the bible of Astrology in Western Europe today. It would appear that the

Celts did not question the meanings of the earlier Wolof names in Ireland given to place names, rivers and harbours and were probably too busy marking their own signatures in their developing technologies on 'the isles'. They may have had their own Celtic Tiger then. The Senegalese tribes brought with them their seafaring skills and boat craftsmanship and fishing.

Thus Irish is made up of mindsets that empowered itself from the heavens and the seas with a moderation for breeding animals and fishing and with a touch of state sponsored Blarney. All this would not have happened had primitive man not pursued the flight path of The Puffin. This colourful bird has been underestimated both in Irish and British culture today and never understood. Yet its name has marked various islands all along its Atlantic path from Africa to Iceland either as a Sea Parrot or a Duck and included Canary Island (Spain), Puffin Island (Ireland & Wales) and Lundi Island (Iceland & Bristol Channel). Their seasonal presence in Senegal and their eating habits intrigued the local Black Africans and thus their quest to follow their trail. This colourful bird is easy to follow because it flies low and stops to eat and remains close to land.

Even in early Christianity Irish Monks on Skellig Rock Island, Kerry gave recognition to its white plumage and saw them as their 'little brothers'. This island was a source of parables of the bible thus the name. Scéal/Carraig – Skellig. These Irish Monks on Skellig Rock Island, Kerry gave recognition to is white plumage and saw them as their 'little brothers'. This island was a source of parables of the bible thus the name. These Irish Monks subsequently were subdued by the beauty of this bird and like homo sapiens also followed its path directly to Iceland bringing with them Christianity, early Brehon Laws and Sagas (our stories).

PTOLMEY'S MAPS

The great geographer Ptolemy (ad 100-180), writing in the library of Alexandria in Egypt, compiled an atlas of the known world. Ireland and Britain (The Isles) were part of his works then. In Ireland he lists 53 names. Their sources are neither reliable nor verifiable and are mainly hearsay from merchants from Britain and given to the Romans were it was gathered by Philemon in the first century. They were then recorded in Latin by Marinus of Tyre. Subsequently generations after generations of scribes preserved it even though they did not understand it and in the process some names became distorted beyond recognition.

There are no books written recording accurately the meaning of any of these names and where an effort was made it failed miserably and in doing so failed in their efforts to explain the origin of the Gaelic language. The Irish Academic Department in Trinity College Dublin is like a Eunuch that castrates the virility of the life the original, native language has to offer.

In this compendium I have attempted to explain seven of those words and maybe more if I had more time.

Senegal & Gambia

This part of Africa is one of the most developed regions in the third world and this has been endorsed by the EU and supported by significant trade between their sponsors. The Wolof language is the most spoken native language in the region and spoken by up to 15 million people including Mauritania.

From the compiled dictionary in this book the similarities of many ancient Gaelic words continue to be shared today.

This dictionary is a substrate language to Gaelic as spoken in Ireland and its source derives from spoken Wolof today from words selected that would have been known to have been in existence since records began. Wolof has changed since it was originally first used by ancient primitive man and may have lost many of its old words once used at that time of the original migration to Ireland. Great efforts have been made not to include modern words and others that have been influenced by the French language. It may be necessary to seek further similarities with other family members in the Niger region namely Manduka, Fula, and Kimwii and to include from Europe Galician, Basque and Portuguese. This study should be a new revelation.

The Wolof people were also referred to as the Atlantic Tribe thus proving how they were seafaring and skilled in boatmanship and fishing.

The Senegal River in West Africa has been that area that represents 'the past', where those homo sapiens left by boat to create the Kingdom of Kerry on the isles. In a strict sense this past does not exist. It is a memory or residue of things that now exist in the present moment, a mental construction - that cleaned up or embellished – often serves the needs of the current moment instead of corresponding to any historic 'truth'. History is bunk, yet it holds extraordinary powers to stir up emotions. Societies that fail to deal adequately with their past seem, like people, to become ill. Why did communism in China end up producing so many features of these centralised bureaucracies of the imperial dynasties it wanted to dismantle? The past isn't dead. It isn't even past. Homo sapiens were more burdened by that past after developing their oral traditions and much of their time was taken up by learning and memorising the traditions, oral poetry, and incantations of their ancestors, even though in many ways they are more present-minded than more written cultures. Early Gaelic had no past tense. This is not the same that they had no sense of the past. For oral societies, the distant past is necessary and indistinct continuum.

History as we understand it begins with writing by making an object outside ourselves to separate us from the past. The tablet carved stone of 'Sile na Gig' and the ogham stones represent this earliest form on the 'isles'. After the agricultural revolution, the technology of writing was served to manage the husbandry of farming and fishing. It had the magical properties – the ability to stop time and preserve things for eternity. Sometimes their tablet of stone omitted a part of the body in case it might jump out and attack them.

When homo sapiens first arrived in the Kingdom of Kerry from the Senegal River, they had no Gods in their universe, no nations, no money, no human rights, no laws, and no justice outside the common imagination of human beings. They cemented their social order by believing in ghosts and spirits and following the movement of the moon.

Modern business people and lawyers are in fact, powerful sorcerers and tell stranger tales than primitive shamans did.

Money isn't a material reality – it is a psychological construct. It works by converting matter into mind. It is the trust that makes money an efficient system.

THE HUMAN JOURNEY

Over 160,000 years ago modern humans homo sapiens lived in Africa. Four groups went their separate ways and of those one went to the Congo basin and then on to the Senegalese River area where they could no longer travel north by foot due to the severity of the Sahara desert.

While man elsewhere continued to travel east and north onwards along the fertile Nile River those along the Senegalese river remained there as their river flowed in an east west direction only. There they developed and created their own new technologies initially from wood and subsequently stone and mastered the art of seafaring skills and boat building. During this time they developed a strong seafaring boat known as The Gaal.

They then travelled to Ireland and Europe by sea and arrived there first before white man did. They were few in number and built Dun Aengus a then circular stone fortification which was then further inland. The Isles of Ireland and Britain were when one huge landmass and embraced the submerged Porcupine Basin off the coast of Kerry. More than 100,000 years ago a magnificent earth disruption occurred and much of the land along the west coast then became lost to the sea leaving what now remains a semi circle of Dun Aengus perched at the side of a high rugged cliff. This was the beginning of time marked by man and nature and remains to this day.

Following a subsequent Ice Age 50,000 years ago these people died out only to be followed by another arrival but this time in larger numbers than before.

Following another Ice Age 25,000 years ago many of those may have died and those that survived did so along the Kerry Coast due to its unique warmer climate and became sallow in complexion. The climate returned to normal 5,000 years later and by then their population had increased and more joined them from the Iberian Peninsula.

Traffic between Senegal and 'The Isles' increased rapidly via Iberia. It was 10,000 years later that white man eventually arrived to 'The Isles' from the Continent.

Hunters Law of Nature

Primitive men hunted to live and were members of a tribe that held their own laws with respect and enforced then with dignity. Their laws also extended to animals too and fair play was their game.

When man arrived from Africa to Ireland they had two unwritten words that were etched in their hunting mindsets. These were 'Taxa' and 'Can'.

It is interesting that both of these words are currently legislated in Ireland/Éire and the only county in the world that legislates each together and separately in the two official languages of The State namely English and Gaelic. This may seem accidental, however it is an 'accidental fact' that could be their national salvation.

Each of the two words have different intentions as you will have found in an earlier chapter even if it is not the intention of any of the Irish ministers for finance. It was the intention of the Tribesmen. There legislation was the original on the isles.

Does that mean that a taxation liability can be less depending on which language you chose to be taxed in 'the state' and/or whether you are fluent in Irish or not? Can the Revenue Appeal Commissioner accept the original meanings coined by these African tribesmen? Does a faux pas by The State over ride the proper meaning?

Will the intentions of the African tribesmen over 50,000 years ago form evidence in law and act as a precedence and maybe save the taxpayer millions/billions of euros in tax if those words can be demonstrated to be relevant today and by extension dismiss claims by the banks against the borrowers? Can the Tribesmen be the new fiscal regulators where many state appointments have been proven to have slept while ' in situ'

The tectonic plates of this academic challenge could change everything for all the Irish Taxpayers/Borrowers and maybe bring back all the Irish Emigrants home again. Is this plausible?

These tall skinny black men did arrive on 'The Isles' and they did use words that are currently legislated by The State. We should make it our business to know what that means now. Today their wisdom might be our national salvation.

Let's mount the forum and introduce these sample words as currently used and examine the intentions of these ancient tribesmen as follows:

Taxation: This means 'To Stick'. These men used wood then as a tool and a weapon to kill animals. 'To Stick' – therefore evokes completely and thoroughly and this is what the minister for finance has in mind when enacting The Finance Acts every year. His enactments are terminal in this instance as we know it. Thus the hunter is present when he delivers the fatal weapon (demand for tax); and

Cain Ioncaim: This means 'To Be Stucked' (to set a trap). This is the past of 'To Stick'. This evokes the speed of thought and time and the oratory skills of the taxpayer and maybe the bank borrower. Thus the hunter is not present when the weapon entraps the taxpayer and the taxpayer/borrower has time to call for help. By extension 'there is a chance' with more time to favour the taxpayer and or the borrower before the hunter returns to his snare. Maybe Appeal Commissioners/Ombudsmen did walk the Savannahs in an ancient time. Perhaps we should count on all of them and claim them to be our own instead of the hunter i. e. minister/bankers. Sore o Can (Wolof) – to be far and away from being stucked and 'Saor ó Cain' (Gaelic) (free of tax) now has a new meaning for all of us. Let us use it instead of taxation/ austerity measures.

Primitive man understood the Laws of Nature that an entrapped animal could escape while awaiting for them to return to their prey.

The ministers for finance on 'the isles' currently depicts their fiscal legislation from mundane hours of contrivance taken to create it rather than undertaking the task of proper judgement and inspiration that will effect this chance as apt to adopt what must now count as the 'intention' by primitive man and not deny fellow citizens their basic rights to a good name by preventing the enforcement upon the weak a cannibalistic interpretation that should otherwise be their own salvation.

Homo Sapiens on the isles of Ireland and Great Britain practiced their humane intentions that needed no interpretation because theirs were already the product of one.

Black America

Black Human Migration from Africa to America began in the same place where more than 100,000 years earlier had initially migrated as free men directly to Europe.

In the beginning Black man arrived to that area in the west of Africa near the Senegalese River and found they could not travel any further by foot. The Sahara desert prevented them. They would have arrived there about 150,000 years ago only to stay on the coastal area of Senegal. They had originally left many thousands of years earlier from lower central Africa known as 'the cradle of mankind'.

They developed seafaring skills by building boats and in due course their technologies became the best and most advanced. They were skilful in hunting and fishing. In their catch they caught the Sea Parrott known as the Puffin. A colourful visible seafaring bird that flew low and only along the Atlantic and migrated to Ireland and Iceland along the west coasts. Initially they had noticed that foods it had eaten were not available locally and every year the Puffins left to return again once more. Finally one day they decided to follow the path of this colourful bird and to hunt further afield. And they did.

Their boat was known as The Gaal meaning a tribal family boat to hunt with. It had a design that suited the wild seas of the ocean and held an uplift bow to challenge the high waves. They were able to sea hunt during their crossings. Many boats left and some arrived directly in Ireland and others to Portugal and Galicia in

Northern Spain. When they arrived to Ireland the Shannon Estuary became their home and they named the Shannon as Senos meaning 'our river' and called after their Senegalese River that also shared the same name and mindset.

They were primitive, their words were few and their tools were made from wood. Nevertheless these men gave the first known names to the Irish Landscape and began the first technologies in Ireland by designing new boats to navigate the Estuary and local rivers. They also formulated the first unwritten words in the laws and nature that would eventually evolve into The Brehon Laws that subsequently formed the basis for The Magna Carta in Britain and subsequently the enactment of the American Bill of Rights now displayed on Capitol Hill. It is only fitting that a copy of The Brehon Laws should also be displayed there too.

Currently Irish and most EU citizens have lost their direct representation to make decisions that matter by allowing the laws of Code Napoleon dictate all decisions made by faceless unelected leaders and bureaucrats. This should be revisited again and civility and trust should be built again from the grass root to the top. The legacy of these primitive people is invaluable.

Who would have believed that up to 100,000 years later black man was forced to migrate from the same places in Senegal. This time as slaves in shackles to the Americas and in boats from designs that their ancestors had once built and some sold by their same long lost cousins and now white from 'the isles of Britain and Ireland. One Black American President family history shared this experience and one of those places was Isles de Goree – a small island off Senegal meaning the island of honourable and honest people situated a short distance off the coast.

In the Americas it is now understandable why tap dancing evolved from meeting native Irish there and how the making of crooked legs (Irish Dancing) became their passion.

Today this past isn't dead. It is not even past.

TAXATION – BRIEF 1 & 2

TAXATION BRIEF 1

We need to know the primal meaning of this word to make good the void our nation is in now.

Taxation from its primitive origins in real jungle economics means 'to capture and bring back to the village the spoils of the hunt'. It would have been consumed immediately. In those days the victim was a wild animal. No victim was allowed to escape the claws of the hunter once caught. This is what Fiscal Taxation is today when The Minister delivers The Demand, 'to Pay'.

Subsequently primitive man evolved into husbandry and farming where the death and the consumption of the animal was postponed to a future date and or provided periodic benefits during their lifetime e.g. milk to consume with new life.

Our Finance Acts need to reform to include more aspects of fiscal husbandry to entice the better farming of the nations finances on the isles and to allow proper wealth bearing companies to make contributions in a more balanced social context to the community where it is domiciled. Jungle economics before conventional religion did not practice the adoration of its victim because it would be expensive to maintain. The State should do the same and share the spoils of its victim with the people as they did at 'Puck Fair'.

In our secular state the division with religion is coded in law to separate the two. Likewise the State should continue this practice in economics and prevent the practice of adoration of false Gods (e.g. Tax Inversions) that will only contribute to our nation demise.

TAXATION BRIEF 2

Blood & Tears

Taxation is a primal activity with the intention 'To Stick' in the presence of 'The Enforcer' (The Hunter).

Sometimes 'The Enforcer' is not present when the 'Tax Payer' (Beast of Prey) becomes entrapped (Notice of Estimation) in a snare (Discover) that is located 'Away'.

The Snare is usually the location that draws the remote Taxpayer into its Territory (Taxable Activity).

A Humane Hunter allows the beast of prey to call for help when entrapped and to choose anyone (Appeal Commissioner/Bank Ombudsman) to assist in being released. Our own River Dog (Minister for Finance) is not humane and instead chooses His Appeal Commissioner/Ombudsman to endure the taxpayer to suffer a further fate of needless pain.

The GREED of the code used by the Irish Minister clouds his ability to think clearly and his efforts to lay claim to the continued existence of an agreed Tax System between the various Hunters (Vested foreign countries) on the spoils of the Beasts of Prey will only cause the elimination of The Territory for our Minister to legislate on. Then our emperor will have no clothes.

Welcome to the Land of the River Dogs.

Back to the Beginning

History of mankind shows that disease and migration influenced the decline and emergence of a language e.g. 'The Plague' – French/English. War can be included and this is usually assisted by ' new technology' of the day. In recent times political union such as the EU has influenced migration significantly in Europe and it remains to be seen how this development impacts on the local language. Religious beliefs have also become visible through migration and in some cases their beliefs and their language are inseparable as in Islam/Arabic.

Currently new technology is the forerunner in communications either in the home/office or as a tourist. Companies such as Facebook, Alibaba and Twitter on one hand, and Ryanair have shown great dexterity in maintaining faster and greater communications between all cultures. This will continue to grow and more new companies will copy their successes. Speed is the weapon.

The Irish language is a cultural subordinate of the English language because the claimants to this freedom to speak this language namely 'the Irish', have chosen so, because they speak English as their working language at home and in the office. Their collective dismissal of Irish/Gaelic where it really matters will only accelerate the final demise of their ancient tongue.

Unlike other European countries the Irish as a viable living community have never professed the freedom to speak Irish and their sovereign republican tenets have chosen through schooling a strict enforcement that has met with a collective rejection from its citizens who are predominately of recent immigrants to the country of less than 200 years ago and whose ancestors never spoke Irish before. The State continues to purvey Irish round its fiefdom (it has lost its economic sovereignty) while at the same time has assisted the domination of its warlord banks and financial overlords and supporting this in legislation. It is no wonder why so many young qualified professionals leave the country to be replaced by new foreigners that will represent the majority in a few years time. This is liken to the sow that eats its young.

Every language has its own colour and flavour: Arabic's austere grandeur and egalitarianism; Chinese unshakeable self regard; Sanskrit's luxuriating classifications and hierarchies; Greek's self confident innovation leading to self obsession and pedantry; Latin's self civil sense; Spanish rigidity, cupidity and fidelity; French admiration for rationality; and English admiration for business acumen. All that can be said for the Irish language is Feck, Music and Dance… and Drink. This indicates the language in the present republic is not meant to be spoken.

Unlike the Irish the Jews are returning to Israel in increasing numbers and professing Hebrew as their living/working language and their Jewishness because they face increase hostility elsewhere in other countries, not withstanding that Israel is surrounded by hostile countries. Economic success follows their path and the Israeli economy continue to prosper. Their attitude to their language embraces and bonds their nation as one unit to remain united in the face of austerity.

Irish Law can adapt and embrace more than it currently legislates and re-invent new principles of Brehon Laws once practiced prior to the enforcement of English Common Law. It is interesting to know that this body of law was the purveyor of the Magna Carta in England. This prestige could initiate a pride in the use of the Irish language and instigate a revival. It can also give pride and security to the HQ of large international companies to chose Ireland as their total legal center of international trade and tax practices and bring Ireland to a world stage who's size would be disproportionate to its new power and enshrine the might of a new superpower.

Irish Law can create a new estate of empowerment where it can only be a win win situation for the nation by claiming absolute ownership of all human data of its citizens especially medical information that can hold value in the real commercial and scientific world.

It remains to be seen can the role of Irish/Gaelic take a new meaning and like the Irish Monks/Scribes in their sacred monasteries hold leadership in large new technology companies and induce the language into a new techno savvy usable language to a wider world using original Irish/Gaelic that can be substrate to a new experience where no man has gone before. After all, primitive man learned from the monkey and coined their words which were the purveyor of the Gaelic/Irish language.

GLOSSARY

Substrate Language: It is an indigenous language that contributes words or parts of speech to the language of an invading people who have imposed their language on the indigenous people. Throughout the United States for instance there are towns with Native American names because Native American languages form a substrate to American English.

Wolof is a substrate to language to Gaelic which can be found in the enclosed compendium.

Wolof is also a substrate to English and that requires a separate study.

DA WU YU CODE (EXTRACT FROM THE BOOK)

The Code of Before Time and After Time

Imagine if waking up some morning and you are living in a time machine that has morphed you back more than 140,000 years and you are to join dotted lines on a return journey to the future that is Now. It is an image because you cannot name or phrase anyone with those human thoughts because they apply to a perceptible being, You.

For this exercise you are standing beside 'The Rock of the Candle' in, Clarina, Co. Limerick, Ireland. The megalithic stone was placed there by ancient man more than 50,000 years ago for the purpose of generating the life force energy of the communities in a land that they loved. This stone has been and still is part of an ancient national mapping process that connects with that energy grid on the island of Ireland and reflects the heavenly gardens in the cosmic universe.

One such grid location is Dun Aengus on the Aran Islands, Galway Bay. Imagine touching the rock and feeling the magic of 'The Rock of the Candle' and closing your eyes and in a moment knowing your soul transcending your life forces across and out into the ocean to this man made gravity and meeting your sub consciousness that you call Dee Noblesse, an ancient dark rugged grey stone on a windswept landscape in The Burren, Co. Clare that in another time was then a mighty power in all its glory and technology.

This is the beginning of your outer body experience that will empower you to new heights with a mystic thought. Your journey has begun into a past of a, before time, known as 'Wu' to a destination of now, an after time, known as 'Yu'. Your diary begins to record that journey and in that experience it is being etched on your soul. Your dream is both a trilogy and a trinity within you with reverence, and what follows is recounted and witnessed by You.

Upon your arrival (refer to maps) your feeling of presence at the ring fort on the Aran Islands is one of before it was built; there was nothing. This period before man marked the earth was before time as we know it. Before time and throughout time, there has been a self-existing being – eternal, infinite, complete, omnipresent. This being cannot be named or phrased, because human speech only applies to perceptible beings.

Walking around the ring fort you can only sense that the primordial being was primitively and, is still, essentially imperceptible. Outside this being, before the beginning, there was nothing "non-being" or "formless", "mystery" or "the principal".

The period when there was not yet any sentient being, when the essence alone of the principal existed, is called "before Heaven"(Wu).

The day that the ring fort was build marked the beginning of Time. From that day the principal was named by the double term of "Heaven and Earth" (Yu). The Heaven and Earth binomial emits all existent sentient beings. The new landscape shaped by man with the ring fort pointed the beginning of the "virtue of the Principal" – i.e. generates all products that fill up the world as we now call it the Gross National Product. The symbol of this landscape can be seen as man's quest to produce, to engage in commerce, and to initiate the faculty of human awareness, rest and activity, or to put it another way, empty and full. The location of this earth's symbol tapped into the earth's energy, life force of the planet, and manifested from this powerful force the power of the human mind to create ideas with images and be moved by passion.

The moment at which this landscape marked the principal of "Heaven and Earth" was the age of Taurus. The landscape also marked part of that area that was known before as the Land of Atlantis. Today the ring fort has lost part of itself to the sea. That part which it has lost has been returned by nature to "The Principal", the period when there was not any sentient being, when there was nothing, when the essence was "before heaven" and when there was no time. The existing structure is a design crafted in partnership by both man and nature. The removal of that part now lost to the sea marks in man's consciousness the period of timelessness when the mind was absolutely still, completely empty and calm. A pure and clear mirror, it was capable of reflecting and ineffable and un nameable essence of the Principal itself. This is called the "Greater Circle".

The middle of the original manmade circular ring fort shows on one part the landscape on which it was originally built and on the other the drop of the high rugged cliffs over the powerful ocean to which it was returned by nature. That part returned to nature also shows to us the altruism of water.

Looking down from the top of the dangerous cliff and in the centre of the original ring fort, your emotions flee from the heights at which it concentrates to the depths below and does not feel idle doing so day or night. Above form the rain and dew, and all around a feeling of purification. Now you look out across the Atlantic Ocean and feel your thoughts become deeper and cohesive with insight and a longing to the past to connect to a line on the waters before you, to an unknown location that is a place that will be reawakened again and the life of the rugged stones around you will reveal once more in chorus the power of Now from an unchanged world bringing to you its music and stories. You are now empowered in ways that you never knew from a life within.

From the centre inland the remaining manmade ring fort the inclination is quite the opposite and the passion to benefit oneself and make profit proliferates your soul to generate wealth. The flesh being wiser than the intellect, this feeling of greatness is in the blood. Your mind can go wrong, but what your blood feels and believes in is always true. These are the unconscious feelings and wanting, not knowing. The essence of this moment at this location is to feel good and useful to all to obey and never resist to stop if confronted by a barrage and to flown when the gate opens. It is a feeling of adaptability to anything.

There is no visible sign left to show how or why the ring fort was parted within itself and no recorded tale to such event. Nonetheless, news did reach Plato subsequently of a land of magnificence in Atlantis. The land of the greater land of Aran, Inis Mor... Ireland... eerand... the land in the west... or Westland and the Land of Tory. The maps of Ireland created by the great Greek Philosopher Ptolemy show Senos, the ancient river now known as the Shannon, and Gangani that part of Corcamore/Newtown (across the river from Shannon Airport) where all the first boats arrived and settled in 'The Isles' and has given its name to the current local boat the 'Gandelow'. The confluence of all people that arrived into that part of the world came from the original migration of man from Africa, since The Great Change, to reach the greater hinterland of Ireland and Inis mor, and continues to the present day.

Before Dun Aengus was destroyed man came from the west. The cause of the shift of the earth's rotation (The Great Change) seemed initially to be cosmic from the Heavens and destroyed the life of the quasar emitting rocks (Quasi-stellar) on the earth's surface, thus causing a massive central deep vaulted rift line in the Atlantic and the Pacific. Time changed forever at that moment. At the time of the beginning of the Age of Taurus and up to and after the ring fort was originally built, the earth's energy revolved on its axis from east to west and Ireland, or more appropriately the greater hinterland of the then Ireland, the Land of Atlantis, was the land in the East. Thus, the confluence of people came west to Atlantis from the Americas and developed their world of Atlantis that has since been lost to mankind.

REFERENCES

Linguistics. (n. d.). Retrieved 08 25, 2015, from http://www. linguistics. ucla. edu/publications/OPL_19. pdf

Wollof. (2005). Retrieved 08 25, 2015, from African Culture: http://www. africanculture. dk/gambia/ftp/wollof. pdf

www. bradshawfoundation. com. (n.d.). Retrieved 08 25, 2015, from http://www. bradshawfoundation. com/stephenoppenheimer/index. php

Some maps provided by Google images.